DMU 0418981 01

AF805098

The Context of Judicial Activism

The Context of Judicial Activism

The Endurance of the Warren Court Legacy in a Conservative Age

FREDERICK P. LEWIS

ROWMAN & LITTLEFIELD PUBLISHERS, INC.
Lanham • Boulder • New York • Oxford

DE MONTFORT UNIVERSITY
LIBRARY (64)
Acc. No.
Date 9/7/99
Loc./Form ~~341.75471~~
Class ~~347.30726~~ 347.3035
LEW

ROWMAN & LITTLEFIELD PUBLISHERS, INC.

Published in the United States of America
by Rowman & Littlefield Publishers, Inc.
4720 Boston Way, Lanham, Maryland 20706

12 Hid's Copse Road
Cumnor Hill, Oxford OX2 9JJ, England

Copyright © 1999 by Frederick P. Lewis

All rights reserved. No part of this publication may be reproduced, stored in a retrieval system, or transmitted in any form or by any means, electronic, mechanical, photocopying, recording, or otherwise, without the prior permission of the publisher.

British Library Cataloguing in Publication Information Available

Library of Congress Cataloging-in-Publication Data

Lewis, Frederick P.
The context of judicial activism : the endurance of the Warren Court legacy in a conservative age / Frederick P. Lewis
p. cm.
Includes bibliographical references and index.
ISBN 0-8476-8991-3 (cloth : alk. paper). — ISBN 0-8476-8992-1 (pbk. : alk. paper)
1. United States. Supreme court. 2. Political questions and judicial power—United States. 3. Warren, Earl 1891–1974. I. Title.
KF8748.L44 1999
347.73'26—dc21
98-17901
CIP

Printed in the United States of America

∞™ The paper used in this publication meets the minimum requirements of American National Standard for Information Sciences—Permanence of Paper for Printed Library Materials, ANSI Z39.48–1984.

Contents

Preface

My motivation in writing this book stemmed initially from a frustration with many of the books that were written about judicial activism in the 1970s and 1980s. Their focus on normative analysis of the exercise of judicial power in a democracy struck me as increasingly futile and uninteresting. My hope is that pointing out here what I believe are some often-neglected realities and important perspectives will prove useful and thought provoking for scholars and students of the field.

Portions of several sections of these chapters have appeared elsewhere in earlier forms, particularly in papers presented at scholarly and professional meetings. Much of chapter six appeared in a paper presented at a national meeting of the American Political Science Association.

Many people offered encouragement as I wrote this book. Of particular note was the support of Richard Morgan of Bowdoin College. Dick disagrees with much of my thesis and argument, and at a time when so many academics confine their thinking and support to the like-minded, those willing to reach out across the bounds of ideology deserve special praise.

This book has benefited significantly from those readers who were kind enough to provide me with many constructive suggestions, and the patient proofreading of Mary Bearden. The responsibility for its remaining deficiencies is mine.

Introduction

The twentieth century has seen two great periods of Supreme Court activism. The first, which continued out of the last decades of the nineteenth century, involved the conservative Court's development of constitutional doctrine to protect business and property. In essence, during this period the Court actively and frequently undertook to frustrate state legislative, and then congressional efforts, to regulate the economy and to ameliorate the economy's harsher effects through social welfare measures.

This period of activism came to an abrupt end and was reversed following the Court-packing crisis of 1936-37. The result has come to be seen as a kind of "settlement" that has been adhered to by conservatives and liberals alike in the ensuing decades. Consequently, most matters of economic policy in America have been removed from the constitutional sphere, and conflicts over them are played out within the "ordinary" political sphere.[1]

The second great period of activism, and the one that is the object of concern here, is appropriately associated with the chief justiceship of Earl Warren. Of course, the identification of an era of Supreme Court activity with its chief justice is primarily just an historian's convenience. A president appoints and removes his cabinet at will and

---

1. See *Wickard v. Filburn,* 317 U.S. 11 (1942). This case illustrates the postcrisis doctrinal activism that gives enormous scope to congressional power and, reciprocally, so restricts the Court's role as to make pointless a judicial challenge to most subsequent congressional regulatory efforts in the social and economic areas. Neither the recent 5-4 decision rejecting the use of the commerce power to support a congressional ban on possession of handguns near public schools, nor the Court's similar rejection of the provisions of the Brady Bill requiring background checks by local officials, seems likely to threaten the "settlement" over economic matters. See *U.S. v. Lopez,* 514 U.S. 549 (1995); *Printz v. U.S.,* 117 S.Ct. 2365 (1997).

his one vote "outvotes" all the others. That is not the case with a chief justice who has but one of nine votes and no real say over who serves with him.

It is true that Earl Warren did not personally agree with every decision of the Court over which he presided. Despite this and the fact that activist efforts associated with his name have "roots" in decisions of the Court made before his time and some "blossoming" that came after his departure, the Warren Court is in fact a fair shorthand for the peak period of extensive liberal activism that broadened, extended, and nationalized civil liberties and civil rights in America in midcentury. This period of judicial activism dramatically altered American constitutional doctrine amid great, acrimonious, and still on-going controversy.

In seeking the underlying meaning of this controversy, I make in this book a number arguments about the subject and all of them too are likely to be controversial. The first is that the activism associated with the "Warren Court revolution," though subjected to strenuous attack and vigorous efforts at judicial counter-revolution over two decades, has survived and prevailed in many of its most fundamental doctrinal aspects, and that thinking about what these are and why this should be is a matter of importance and interest. I attempt to delineate what I think these fundamental doctrinal aspects are and then consider how their survival leads to further issues.

My second argument is that most recent writing about judicial activism, which focuses on normative analysis of the exercise of judicial power in a democracy, is increasingly futile and uninteresting. I suggest that this approach is incapable of resolving the normative dilemma upon which the effort is premised, and that it has reached a point of diminishing intellectual returns.

The third argument is that there is a context within which judicial activism occurs and which often shapes it. That context is multifaceted with ideological, political, historical, and societal aspects. Considering activism in its broad context is a potentially more fruitful approach to the subject. Accordingly, I suggest there is a relationship between the Court's activity and the broader intellectual context, though the precise cause and effect relationship is difficult to determine. I further suggest that the recent normative scholarly effort can be understood as part of the intellectual context of the effort to reverse Warren Court era achievements.

Considering the activism in political context lends a number of helpful insights and, concretely, Warren Court era affirmative remedies are illuminated when they are considered as phenomena that occurred in a broad contemporary bureaucratic and institutional context. More fundamentally, I suggest that the survival and acceptance of Warren Court doctrinal innovation can be best understood when it is considered within a developing broad historical and social context.

Considering the activism within such a context leads to my fourth argument, that judicial activism is a form of creative constitutional development, and that the practice of making such necessary or useful constitutional adjustments of dubious formal legitimacy has been a characteristic of the British and American constitutional systems for centuries. I hold that the tendency in America to engage in this practice is not limited to the judiciary but has become focused there because of the judiciary's claim to constitutional supremacy, and that at some level, efforts at creative constitutional development are on-going.

The fifth argument is that an effort at creative constitutional development, including the form that occurs through the practice of judicial activism, is likely to succeed or fail depending on the appropriateness of its "fit" within this always changing and developing context, particularly the underlying social context. A successful fit with the context in the broadest sense means that the central doctrinal innovations of the activism are likely to be enduring and become accepted as legitimate in the long run despite the inevitable, and in some sense always justified, criticism of them as an exercise of raw power. A poor fit suggests they will be transient.

Concretely, I concede that there may well be elements of specific doctrines promulgated by the Warren Court that reflect the ideological beliefs of particular justices then sitting and which can be judged today as idiosyncratic, time-bound, or wrongheaded in some way. Nevertheless, I argue that despite the enormous controversy that resulted from the Warren Court's work, the survival and acceptance of the fundamental doctrinal developments of the Warren Court era result from its largely successful effort to accommodate a newly developing pattern of pluralism in America, while working to dismantle an older pattern. As a result, a struggle has been generated between the two patterns and their adherents, which frequently focuses on the elements of judicial doctrine that has facilitated the newer pattern.

In conclusion, I consider what kind of judicial activism is most likely to succeed over time. I also examine the confluence of factors that support and in turn facilitate the overall thrust of the activism of the Supreme Court in recent decades, and finally, I consider likely future trends and the long-term outlook for the specific accomplishments of the Warren Court revolution. Despite the intense conflict and occasional changes in doctrine that have occurred and will occur, I expect both the newer pattern of pluralism and the generation of facilitating judicial doctrine to continue to develop over the coming decades.

one/Judicial Activism

The practice of judicial review has always been both controversial and awkward within the American system. As democracy developed within the nation and its political institutions, the claims of judicial review frequently seemed anomalous. Over the course of two centuries, the Supreme Court has successfully asserted that it and it alone has the final say on the constitutionality of the actions of the elected branches of national government and all branches of state government. Since the difficulties involved in amending the Constitution are so great, this means that under normal circumstances, five out of nine persons appointed for life effectively have the last word on what is and is not legitimate governmental action in America. Understandably, this strikes many people as a peculiar arrangement for a nation that claims to be a democracy.

The traditional rationale that has been put forward, either explicitly or implicitly, involves the notion that judicial review is properly understood as at heart, a technical process. Supreme Court justices are seen as expert lawyers who engage in a technical, expert "lawyer" activity. After all, the Constitution is the supreme law of the land and the process of judicial review is a process whereby laws, and other actions of governmental authority that should be under law, are reviewed for their conformance or non-conformance with this supreme law of the land. This conception of review can accept that some justices may occasionally fall short of the professional ideal, but it would see these instances as exceptions to the rule or perhaps as resulting from inevitable human imperfections that arise in striving toward an essentially achievable goal. Certainly this is a view of judicial review which, when accepted, does tend to confer overall legitimacy.

While sophisticated opinion has always been somewhat skeptical of this rationale, in recent decades such skepticism has become more widespread in American society. To understand why, one need merely hypothesize a trip to the hospital for a pain in one's leg. The first doctor who comes in declares it is a growth in the leg that is causing the pain, and calls for surgery the next day to remove it. A second doctor comes in and declares the source of the pain is a ruptured disc in the vertebrae impacting a nerve that is causing a sensation of pain in the leg; he calls for a back operation. The third doctor agrees that the cause of the pain in the leg lies in the leg, but attributes it to an injured kneecap. Six additional doctors are consulted. When each has made his or her diagnosis, the final tally is five doctors calling for an operation on the leg, and four on the back. And among the five calling for a leg operation, three would seek to remove a growth and two will operate to repair the kneecap. Understandably in such circumstances, one's faith in the technical expertise of the medical profession might be shaken.

Consider now that while such a scenario is hopefully increasingly rare in hospitals, this is roughly what often happens on the Supreme Court when major constitutional issues come before it. The divisions are so sharp, so basic, and so frequent that they cast serious doubt on the proposition that what is going on is fundamentally a technical process.

This is not to suggest that judicial review does not involve some considerable elements of a technical process. Clearly it does and in many situations these elements will limit effectively and significantly the scope and freedom of action available to the Court. But the kinds of division that do appear reveal to all the limitations of the technical process of judicial review.

The implication of many critiques of judicial activism is that activism is something clearly distinct from "ordinary" or "legitimate" judicial review. Even those who defend certain kinds of judicial activism seem to share that debatable premise, and the definitional conflicts that occur tend to be shaped by the protagonists express or implied acceptance of it as well as their acceptance or rejection of several related ideas. In fact, it is highly doubtful that there are many, indeed perhaps any, truly important instances of judicial review that everyone would find unquestionably and completely acceptable and legitimate. Therefore, defining judicial activism simply as illegitimate judicial review or as a dubious tendency that likely and frequently deteriorates into illegitimacy is unhelpful because such definitions are completely subjective. At this point, to facilitate the purposes of this book, a useful definition of judicial activism should be general and to the greatest extent possible, framed in a manner that is not debatable.

Bradley C. Canon defines judicial activism by six delineating dimensions. These include (1) the degree to which policies adopted through democratic processes are judicially negated; (2) the degree to which earlier court decisions, doctrines, or interpretations are altered; (3) the degree to which constitutional provisions are interpreted contrary to the clear intentions of their drafters or the clear implications of the language used; (4) the degree to which the decisions make substantive policy rather than affect the preservation of democratic political processes; (5) the degree to which a judicial decision establishes policy itself as opposed to leaving it to the discretion of other agencies; and (6) the degree to which a judicial decision supersedes serious consideration of the same problem by other governmental agencies.[1]

Canon's effort is commendable for its tone. He undertakes to neither "condemn nor defend" activism saying, "it is simply a fact of judicial life." But for a variety of reasons, many of which are explored in the chapters that follow, there are problems with most of his "dimensions."

Using dimensions one, five, and six as measures of activism ignores the real possibility that other agencies of democratic government may seek to act on a "problem" in a manner that greatly and rather clearly exceeds their appropriate powers. If the Court acts to stop this, is that activism? There is also the problem that if the Court acts to preserve democratic processes under dimension four, which under Canon's definition of that dimension is not activism, such action may well conflict with dimensions one, five, or six, since either the popular majority or some other agency of "democratic" government, may strongly want the policy that in practice would significantly interfere with democratic processes. Dimension three, clear intent and/or clear language, is rarely available to us. That leaves only dimension number two really available as a consistent, reasonably objective and useful measure of activism.

The term activism will be used in this book simply to characterize a Court willing to use its authority to engage in judicial review in an assertive manner. Such assertiveness will also imply here a considerable degree of doctrinal pronouncement that is innovative, at least in the sense that it has not been explicitly pronounced before. The term activist will be employed in opposition to describing a Court as "restrained" in the use of its authority and in the development of doctrine.

---

1. Bradley C. Canon, "Defining the Dimensions of Judicial Activism," *Judiciature* 66, No. 6 (December-January 1983): 236-246.

Judicial restraint in its usual conception involves deference to the established authority and actions of the elected branches of government. It similarly implies a cautiousness about doctrinal innovation. However, doctrinal innovation by the Court that serves to sustain a constitutionally innovative (and therefore, arguably dubious) exercise of authority by a legislature or executive might also reasonably be described as a form of judicial activism. Under this approach, the term activism will be employed without regard to its arguable legitimacy or illegitimacy, or the legitimacy or illegitimacy of the doctrinal innovation in question, since an assertive judiciary engaging in doctrinal innovation will inevitably be accused of illegitimacy by someone.

Such accusations will hold that the sort of assertiveness and doctrinal innovation that merely interprets the Constitution is legitimate, but that assertiveness and doctrinal innovation in the criticized instance goes beyond appropriate interpretation and constitutes illegitimate activism. Defenders will find that the particular instance of assertiveness and doctrinal innovation in question is in fact a manifestation of legitimate interpretation. (One might be tempted to analogize the argument over the implications of even a little assertiveness and doctrinal innovation to that over the implications of being a little bit pregnant, were not the latter quite literally at the center of much contemporary debate over judicial activism.)

From the earliest days of the Republic, the United States Supreme Court has been accused of judicial activism. Chief Justice John Marshall was not the first chief justice, but his career in that position, which began in the nineteenth century, is associated in the minds of most informed Americans with an activist approach to constitutional interpretation. Despite some scholarly dissent, this is an accurate perception.

Marshall explored the potential of the Court within the American system early on. In *Marbury v. Madison*[2] he claimed the exclusive power to interpret the Constitution for the Supreme Court even as to the co-equal branches of the national government. In *McColloch v. Maryland*[3] he struck a double blow for national power. First he enunciated a broad construction of Congress's legislative powers. Then, having legitimated congressional action, he provided a ringing statement of national supremacy over conflicting state law.

2. 5 U.S. (1 Cranch) 137 (1803).
3. 17 U.S. (4 Wheat.) 316 (1819).

Despite this, Wallace Mendelsohn argues that Marshall was not an activist because Marshall did what he was supposed to do. Marshall's nationalist interpretation was in conformance with the intentions of the founding fathers and the document they created, and therefore, he claims, Marshall was not an activist.[4]

In fact, Mendelsohn's claims are debatable. The matter of Marshall's conformance to the intentions of the framers of the Constitution is scarcely as clear-cut as he suggests. But even if it was, the nature, scope, and opportunity for the expression of conforming constitutional doctrine was neither clear nor automatic. Marshall claimed authority and then used it audaciously and creatively where he felt he could. He most certainly was not deferential to legislative authority or restrained in the exercise of his powers where he thought he could get away with asserting them vigorously. For purposes of the analysis here, he most definitely qualifies as an activist chief justice.

Marshall's activism was shaped by the context in which it occurred, and to the extent there was an appropriateness of fit within this context, the activism succeeded by enduring in the long run. Perhaps Mendelsohn's point can be restated to support this point which is really the thesis of this book. The text and intention of the Constitution were scarcely as clear, solid, and understood as Mendelsohn would have it. But there was certainly a developing climate of ideas and social forces that provided a supportive context for much of Marshall's doctrinal activism and innovation. This was particularly true, as has been recognized for generations, over the long run and it accounts for most of Marshall's long-standing reputation for greatness.

Despite Marshall's fame for *Marbury v. Madison* and his vigorous assertion of the power of the Supreme Court to declare acts of Congress unconstitutional, Marshall never again declared an act of Congress unconstitutional though his Court struck down several acts of state legislatures. The next law of Congress to be declared unconstitutional was the Missouri Compromise in *Dred Scot v. Sanford.*[5] This decision, widely viewed as unfortunate, is also widely viewed as judicial activism of the least successful sort.

---

4. Wallace Mendelsohn, "Was Chief Justice Marshall an Activist?" in Halpern and Lamb, *Supreme Court Activism and Restraint* (Lexington, Mass.: Lexington Books, 1982). Another interesting perspective on Marshall, though not perhaps a conflicting one, is that of Leslie Friedman Goldstein. In her book, *In Defense of the Text* (Savage, Md.: Rowman and Littlefield, 1991) she sees Marshall as a "moderate textualist."

5. 60 U.S. (19 How.) 393 (1857).

The *Dred Scot* Court is seen by many as naively having believed that it could settle once and for all the conflict over slavery that was then tearing the nation apart. Needless to say, a developing climate of ideas and social forces to provide a supportive context for the decision was absent. Instead, the Court's intervention only aggravated the volatile political situation and arguably helped bring on the Civil War.

Although *Dred Scot* did great damage to the Court's reputation and to the institution of judicial review, once the Civil War was over, the Court slowly recovered. It was very cautious during the period of congressional dominance during Reconstruction, deferring to Congress in ways still unique in American history. Most notably, in the case of *Ex Parte McCardle,*[6] the Court acquiesced in Congress's removing the Court's appellate jurisdiction over a constitutional issue then about to come before it.

One of the first acts of the post-Civil War Congress was to enact the Thirteenth Amendment to abolish slavery. Shortly thereafter, Congress enacted the Civil Rights Bill of 1866, designed to confer basic civil rights upon the newly freed slaves and eliminate remaining badges of slavery. However, doubts about the act's constitutionality led to the passage of the Fourteenth Amendment. And finally, the desire to extend the franchise to the freedmen produced the Fifteenth Amendment. These amendments were followed by a series of enforcement legislation.

But by the 1870s and 1880s the Court began to systematically undermine the accomplishments of the Reconstruction Congresses. In the *Slaughterhouse Cases,*[7] it rejected the broad construction of the Fourteenth Amendment's privileges and immunities clause that would have made all the traditional rights of free men incidents of national citizenship and provided solid constitutional authority for all reconstruction enforcement legislation. In the *Civil Rights Cases,*[8] the Court held that the equal protection clause reached only state action not private action and that Congress's enforcement powers could not reach discrimination in privately owned places of public accommodation. In *Plessy v. Ferguson,*[9] the Court held that segregated facilities did not violate the command of equal protection.

6. 74 U.S. (7 Wall.) 506 (1869).
7. 83 U.S. (16 Wall.) 36 (1873).
8. 109 U.S. 3 (1883).
9. 163 U.S. 537 (1896).

As the Court began to gut the Fourteenth Amendment as authority for the vindication of the rights of the freedmen, it simultaneously began using the amendment to vest property rights through the development of the doctrine of substantive due process. In so doing, it began the first great lengthy period of judicial activism, now quite thoroughly discredited, that took place in the wake of the post-Civil War industrial expansion and lasted until the mid-1930s.

An America that had been overwhelmingly agrarian gave way to an urbanized, industrial nation. Industrial capitalism and corporate growth made dramatic changes in American society and produced social conditions that began to be perceived in many quarters as serious problems or even as great evils. Gradually, in response to public pressure, some states began to seek to exercise their regulatory authority to ameliorate these difficulties.

In many cases, these regulatory efforts did not succeed easily. The political opposition was sometimes fierce and the struggle often bitter. Increasingly, prevailing social philosophy and legal theory supported laissez faire and opposed regulation. As time passed, it became more the case that even where regulation was achieved and a battle won, the war would not be over. Opponents of regulation increasingly turned to the courts and the Constitution in an effort to define "property rights" broadly and then, by constitutionalizing them, place them beyond the reach of political majorities. These efforts succeeded gradually as the Supreme Court began to listen and then to endorse their arguments. The results were the rise of Substantive Due Process, an insistence on a restrictive view of Congress's powers and ultimately, the Court-packing crisis of 1937.

The attempt to turn the Fourteenth Amendment to the objective of providing an effective device for vesting property rights began early but met initial resistance from the Court. A broad attempt was rejected in *The Slaughterhouse Cases*[10] in 1873. The principal claim that granting a slaughterhouse monopoly interfered with the privileges and immunities of citizens of the United States in violation of the guarantee in the Fourteenth Amendment was disposed of by a narrow 5-4 vote. The majority held that the clause did not expand the scope of rights encompassed by the privileges and immunities clause and the right in question remained an attribute of state citizenship. A subsidiary claim that the monopoly denied petitioners liberty and property without due process of law and so violated the amendment's

10. 83 U.S. (16 Wall.) 36 (1873).

due process clause was disposed of with a description of the clause as a procedural guarantee only.

A challenge to state power to regulate the prices charged by grain elevators was rebuffed in *Munn v. Illinois*[11] with a clear affirmation of the state's traditional power to regulate businesses affected with a public interest. But in *Mugler v. Kansas*[12] the Court emphasized that the due process clause did indeed require that regulation must be reasonable and that it was appropriate for the Court to "look at the substance of things," reviewing the legislature's determination as to its reasonableness--a formulation that seemed to cast the Court in an ultimate legislative role.

Finally in 1890, in *Chicago, Milwaukee, and St. Paul Railway Co. v. Minnesota*[13] the Court used the due process clause to declare a state regulatory law unconstitutional. Reserving to itself the right to inquire into the reasonableness of state regulatory legislation potentially made the Court a third house to every state legislature in the country.

After that it was not a long journey to *Lochner v. New York*[14] where the Court majority found "liberty of contract" among the Fourteenth Amendment liberty and property rights being denied without due process of law by a New York statute that limited the working day of bakers to ten hours. The state's action interfered with the constitutional right of bakery owners and employees to freely contract to work a longer day. This holding occasioned Justice Oliver Wendell Holmes's famous dissent with its assertion that the Fourteenth Amendment does not enact Mr. Herbert Spencer's Social Statics.

The reference was to one of the leading works of the day that expressed a philosophy known as Social Darwinism, which likened social and economic life to the evolutionary survival of the fittest. By providing a rationale for social inequality that suggested it was an inescapable part of the natural order of things, it further implied that governmental action to alter this order was unnatural and futile.

Although the battle over Substantive Due Process was long and hard-fought, there were some occasional victories for the side supporting state regulatory efforts. Among the most notable was Louis Brandeis's achievement in *Muller v. Oregon*[15] where his "Brandeis Brief," filled with factual data, convinced the Court that the special biological role of women justified protective state regulation of their

---

11. 94 U.S. 113 (1877).
12. 123 U.S. 623 (1887).
13. 134 U.S. 418 (1890).
14. 198 U.S. 45 (1905). Justice Holmes's dissent begins at page 74.
15. 208 U.S. 412 (1908).

work day. (This was viewed as a major victory for progressive social forces in its time, however it may look to feminists today.) But these occasional approvals of state regulation only underlined the Court's insistence on serving as the final arbiter of state legislative reasonableness, and many of its judgments remained hostile to the effort to use state power to ameliorate the harsher effects of industrialization.

As the country became more conservative again in the 1920s, Substantive Due Process was applied by the Court with renewed vigor. A law of Congress regulating minimum wages for women in the District of Columbia was found to violate the Fifth Amendment's due process guarantee in *Adkins v. Children's Hospital*[16] in 1923. The Court majority expressed the view that excepting women from the general proscription against minimum hour laws was a form of discrimination no longer warranted in light of the then recent enactment of women's suffrage.

With the onset of the Great Depression in the 1930s, the Court at first signaled a willingness to defer to state regulatory schemes. In 1934 in *Home Building and Loan Association v. Blaisdell,*[17] five justices upheld the Minnesota mortgage moratorium law, which imposed a limited moratorium on mortgage payments. The Court, in the face of a claim that the moratorium violated the Constitution's prohibition against impairment of contracts, said that while an emergency could not create power, it could furnish the occasion for the exercise of power. And in *Nebbia v. New York,*[18] the Court upheld a law in the face of a due process challenge that created a milk control board empowered to set minimum and maximum milk prices.

But in 1936, Substantive Due Process returned in *Morehead v. New York ex rel. Tipaldo*[19] when the Court struck down a minimum wage law. Its persistence in the face of a great national crisis was seen by many as only aggravating the situation. By this time, though, Supreme Court resistance to state regulation was being subsumed in a larger issue.

While state regulatory efforts continued to encounter judicial resistance and the barrier of Substantive Due Process, the limited efficacy of state remedies, even when sustained by the courts, had became increasingly evident. A state law regulating and prohibiting, say, child labor was a cost of doing business that many businesses would

---

16. 261 U.S. 525 (1923).
17. 290 U.S. 398 (1934).
18. 291 U.S. 502 (1934).
19. 298 U.S. 587 (1936).

refuse to bear, and it could be avoided simply by moving the factory to a state without such a law. The felt need was for national regulation of a national economy, and this meant congressional legislation.

In the early decades of this century, battles were played out in Congress over anti-trust, pure food and drugs, child labor, and other issues. Sometimes there was success for reform efforts, but this was invariably followed by judicial challenge. The grounds for the challenge were usually based upon a claim that the Congress's limited, delegated powers under the Constitution were simply inadequate to accomplish the end being sought. These conflicts, particularly those over the reach and proper exercise of the interstate commerce clause, showcased the different analytical approaches to the clause that were to war in the early decades of the century.

The nature of interstate commerce is a matter that lends itself to many perspectives. Perhaps it is helpful to consider interstate commerce as analogous to a piece of movie film. You can look at the film one frame at a time as a series of discrete stills, or you can view it projected on a screen as continuous action. In the early decades of the twentieth century, the Court struggled with the question of whether commerce should be seen as a series of discrete transactions or as an integrated and continuous stream. The first point of view would result in some discrete interstate transactions subject to Congressional regulation and others that were local and not. The second point of view suggested something that seemed to compel regulation as a whole in a systematic manner. The great sticking point with the second perspective, apart from legitimizing many regulatory policies that conservatives could not stomach, was that it left little commerce that could not be reached by Congress. A long tradition suggested that this was a result that could not be.

Thus, the Court refused to sustain a congressional prohibition of goods produced with child labor from interstate commerce.[20] The Court insisted on seeing a series of discrete transactions in the process. Those involving manufacture were local and not subject to congressional regulation. Since child labor occurred during manufacturing, Congress could not reach it directly, and the Court would not let Congress do indirectly what it would not let it do directly.

Similarly, the Court refused to sustain an anti-trust prosecution of the sugar trust in *United States v. E. C. Knight*.[21] Although the actions taken to create a sugar monopoly impacted the entire nation, the Court

---

20. *Hammar v. Dagenhart*, 247 U.S. 251 (1918).

21. 156 U.S. 1 (1895).

insisted that since these "contracts and acts" that were being challenged by the federal government "related exclusively to the acquisition of . . . refineries and the business of sugar refining in" one particular state, they were not in and of themselves interstate commerce and directly subject to the reach of the national government.

On the other hand, the meat packing cases[22] illustrate best the Court's acceptance of a stream of commerce approach. The Pure Food and Drug Act regulation focused on processing plants. While there may be distinctions that can be made between these cases and others, they are scarcely distinctions that had to be made. Why the Court sustained regulation in these cases is debatable (certainly Justices eat meat along with other Americans) but the cases demonstrate that a more "modern" point of view reflecting the realities of a changing, industrialized America was possible.

The recognition of the new realities of commerce might have been expected to make the older distinctions hard to hold to, but the Court persisted. The different points of view continued to coexist until the economic crisis of the Great Depression created a political crisis so serious that it called into question the role of the Court in our system as never before or since.

The onset of the Great Depression in the late 1920s and early 1930s resulted in the election of Franklin D. Roosevelt in 1932 and the New Deal. The extent of the crisis with its massive unemployment created a powerful demand for action. And the New Deal responded with a series of regulatory thrusts that stretched congressional authority. It took time for cases that would challenge these acts to make their way to the Supreme Court, but when they began to arrive, the Court's response was not supportive.

The election of Roosevelt as president with large Democratic majorities in Congress ended an era of Republican dominance. It had begun with McKinley's victory over Bryan in the election of 1896 and was interrupted only by the Woodrow Wilson years made possible when Theodore Roosevelt split the Republicans with his Bull Moose challenge in 1912. But despite the end of one political era and the beginning of another that would dominate American politics for most of nearly four decades, the Supreme Court that lasted into the new era was a product of the previous one. Only three of the nine justices--Brandeis, Cardozo, and Stone, were consistent liberals, and Roosevelt had no chance to appoint a justice during his first four years.

---

22. *Swift v. United States,* 196 U.S. 375 (1905); *Stafford v. Wallace,* 258 U.S. 495 (1922).

Admittedly, the most dramatic rejection, the *Schecter Poultry*[23] case, which struck down the National Industrial Recovery Administration, had important elements in it involving delegation of powers that commanded unanimity on the Court. But other elements did not and as events unfolded these became vital. In *Carter v. Carter Coal Co.*[24] the divided Court struck down congressional efforts to regulate wages and hours and production in the coal industry. The Court insisted on adhering to the point of view that broke commerce up into discrete transactions, some local, some interstate, but with virtually all the matters the president and Congress needed to address defined as local, they were beyond their reach.

Not only did Roosevelt find important parts of his program struck down but even more critical was the fact that truly central parts of his program were coming up for challenge. Given the language of the Court's decisions, it was hard to see how the rest of the New Deal could survive. Among the legislation in danger was the National Labor Relations Act, which legitimized unions and collective bargaining, and the Social Security Act.

It was, of course, not simply the defeat of particular parts of Roosevelt's program that was troubling. By using Substantive Due Process to frustrate state power, the Court was saying that the states lacked the authority under the Constitution to deal with these kinds of extremely serious social problems. By adhering to the narrow construction of the commerce clause and other arguably empowering provisions, it said that Congress too lacked the power. It began to look as if the Court's actions meant that nowhere in the United States's government system did such power practically exist.

It did not seem to matter that a clear majority of the people strongly wanted this kind of action taken. It did not seem to matter that the crisis of the Depression was very extreme, threatening even the continued existence of democracy and constitutional government. It did not seem to matter that Roosevelt and a New Deal Congress had been endorsed by the people in the election of 1936 bringing Roosevelt a victory, then the largest in modern times. It did not seem to matter that in the face of all these other considerations, just six men out of a total of nine, appointed for life, were imposing their constitutional view on America.

But of course it did matter, and in the end, Roosevelt decided he would not stand for it. Strengthened by his re-election, he decided to

---

23. *Schecter Poultry Corporation v. United States*, 295 U.S. 495 (1935).

24. 298 U.S. 238 (1936).

put his mandate into action and deal with what he viewed as an outrageously obstructionist Court.

Roosevelt's Court-packing plan sought to take advantage of the one clear and indisputable loophole in the arrangements that sustain the Supreme Court's counter-majoritarian position in our system. Although the Court's decisions cannot be overturned directly except by constitutional amendment, nor can a justice be removed except by an impeachment that requires two-thirds majority in Congress, the number of justices on the Supreme Court is set by ordinary statute and can therefore be increased by ordinary statute. A determined president and an insistent congressional majority can enact a statute raising the number of justices. This then creates a number of immediate vacancies for the president to fill, thus permitting the prompt appointment of a new majority.

Roosevelt was determined but his party's congressional majority was not so insistent. The support of many for the New Deal was tempered by a serious concern for the checks and balances of the American system. The legislation ultimately was not enacted.

But the Court-packing battle was not the war. As it turned out, the election and the pressure were not without effect. When the decisions in *National Labor Relations Board v. Jones and Laughlin Steel Corporation*[25] came out in early 1937, further efforts to alter the Court's path were made unnecessary. In what contemporary wags called "the switch in time that saved nine," Chief Justice Hughes and Justice Roberts changed from voting for the "conservative" side and a restrictive view of Congress's powers to the other, more expansive side, and the legislation's constitutionality was upheld.

The change was dramatic and in a short time, it became clear that it was permanent and decisive. As the older justices finally began leaving the Court in the late 1930s, Roosevelt's appointees took firm control and consolidated the victory. The Court announced doctrine so broad as to end all judicial involvement in the economic policy arena. No practical restrictions were left on Congress's powers in this area.

A similar decisive reversal took place on Substantive Due Process. The Court announced decisively that henceforth all economic regulatory legislation would be presumed reasonable, that the burden would fall on anyone challenging state legislation to establish that no reasonable basis could be advanced for it, and that if any reasonable basis could be advanced then the law was valid regardless of what the

---

25. 301 U.S. 1 (1937).

justices might think of its wisdom. The Court would not substitute its judgment for that of the state legislature.

The change in the Court's approach to Congress's powers is dramatically illustrated by the case of *Wickard v. Filburn*.[26] Here a farmer challenged the constitutionality of the second Agricultural Adjustment Act as enforced by Secretary of Agriculture Wickard. In addition to planting his wheat quota under the act, Farmer Filburn planted a small additional amount of acreage that he said was for his own use. It might be used to feed his livestock or consumed by his family, but it would not enter interstate commerce. It probably would not enter commerce at all. So how could the federal government regulate it?

The Court held that the federal government could regulate this "extra" acreage on the theory that by growing on this extra land for his own purposes Filburn avoided going to the commercial market for this wheat. And if all farmers did this, it would indeed have a substantial impact on interstate commerce and, as such, could be reached by the national government.

The decision is truly sweeping. It would seem that precious little can escape congressional reach under such a test and analytic approach. Could not Congress stop people from growing vegetables in their home gardens on the theory that by doing so, they avoid going to the supermarket to buy them and consequently substantially impacting on interstate commerce? We cannot be certain, of course, for Congress has never passed such a law and is not ever likely to.

The Court's dramatic change ended the conflict between liberals and conservatives over the propriety of constitutionalizing issues of economic regulation. The "Settlement of 1937" accomplished several things. First it ended Substantive Due Process in the area of state economic regulation. The Court also put forward an interpretation of Congress's power, particularly in the area of regulation of interstate commerce, so broad that some think there are no practical constitutional limits left upon the power, at least within the economic arena. Finally, it had an enormous impact on the issue of judicial activism. An entire generation of scholars were powerfully affected by struggle over whether or not the Court would withstand the strong popular mandate for the New Deal.

The outcome of the Court-packing crisis is referred to here, and elsewhere, as a "settlement" because that is what it has amounted to. No formal meeting was held by conservatives and liberals or a treaty

26. 317 U.S. 111 (1942).

entered into, but the impact historically and institutionally has been as great as if a formal agreement had been made. Indeed, one Supreme Court venture into what many construed as a small shift into reverse was promptly undone by the Court only a few years thereafter.[27]

But the end of one period of judicial activism soon gave rise to another, which many date from the famous "preferred position" footnote in *U.S. v. Carolene Products*.[28] Here the Court, while reiterating the expansive post-settlement view of Congress's powers, suggested in footnote four that the same presumption of validity of legislative enactment might not apply whenever "legislation appears on its face to be within a specific prohibition of the Constitution, such as those of the first ten amendments, which are deemed equally specific when held to be embraced within the Fourteenth."

The footnote also suggested the possibility of greater scrutiny in situations involving legislation "which restricts those political processes which can ordinarily be expected to bring about repeal of undesirable legislation" and "statutes directed at particular religious . . . or national . . . or racial minorities" suggesting that "prejudice against discrete and insular minorities may be a special condition, which tends seriously to curtail the operation of those political processes ordinarily to be relied upon to protect minorities." The now-

---

27. See *National League of Cities v. Usery,* 426 U.S. 833 (1976) and *Garcia v. San Antonio Metropolitan Transit Authority,* 469 U.S. 528 (1985).

Recently in *U.S. v. Lopez,* 514 U.S. 549 (1995), the Court struck down a congressional statute banning possession of a firearm near a public school. The law had been based on the interstate commerce power. The narrow 5-4 majority basically argued that the law involves matters that are neither interstate nor commerce. It seems very unlikely that the case will threaten the "settlement" over Congress's powers to regulate the economy. The dissenting Breyer opinion was vigorous. Indeed, Congress itself has concluded that if it is more careful and does its "homework," it can re-enact this statute with the proper "findings" and pass muster under an interstate commerce theory.

The year 1997 saw an additional "swipe" at national power as the Court struck down that part of the Brady Law that required local law enforcement authorities to perform background checks on would-be gun purchasers. The provision was seen as an improper comandeering of state executive power by the national government, in violation of the Tenth Amendment. *Printz v. United States,* 117 S. Ct. 2329 (1997). However, it still appears that the bare Court majority here, while determined to set limits on national policing power, is not seeking to disturb the economic settlement of the 1930s, and as many observers have pointed out, the change of only one vote on the Court could end even this narrow venture.

28. 304 U.S. 144 (1938).

famous footnote proved to be an accurate description of the policy and philosophy that gradually animated decisionmaking in what can now be seen as a transition period of the 1940s, accelerating in the 1950s, and reaching a peak in the early to mid-1960s Warren Court years.

The period of serious incorporation of the Bill of Rights though the due process clause of the Fourteenth Amendment then began in earnest ultimately making most provisions of the Bill of Rights applicable to the states as well as to the federal government. The doctrinal stress on incorporation seems odd to some observers today and the early arguments over total incorporation versus selective incorporation remind others of theological arguments over matters like partial or total immersion. The issues must be understood in light of the then-recent battle over substantive due process in the economic arena.

Having savaged conservative activists for decades for arbitrarily reading their political and economic philosophy into the Constitution illegitimately, the liberal Roosevelt appointees who now controlled the Court were concerned, to one degree or another, with distinguishing what they were doing from what their opponents had done. Putting aside the merits of the arguments over incorporation, claiming that the due process clause incorporated the Bill of Rights, a nominally specific and unquestionably venerable list, gave at very least an appearance of textual concreteness that could be used to distinguish this venture from that of the predecessor Court. As will be discussed subsequently, the practical result of the multidecade process that culminated in the Warren Court's many controversial decisions was to greatly develop American civil liberties doctrine and then impose national standards upon often recalcitrant state and local governmental authorities.

A related doctrinal development then occurred in the area of equal protection. It can be summed up as simply taking equal protection seriously. As the first Justice Harlan pointed out in his *Plessy* dissent, and as subsequent historical developments proved, "separate but equal" was never a serious proposition. Then by far the poorest part of the country, the South was scarcely in a position to afford one decent set of public facilities, let alone two. And since segregation was a charade masking white beliefs in racial supremacy, no serious effort to provide equality of resources was ever made until the very end in a few places as part of a desperate attempt to salvage segregation.

By subjecting the doctrine of "separate but equal" to serious scrutiny and increasing analytical rigor, the postsettlement Court began a series of thrusts that undermined the doctrine. This effort culminated in *Brown v. Board of Education,* which opened the era of Warren Court activism dramatically and created political and scholarly controversies as least as contentious as those that surrounded the era of Supreme Court activism in the area of economic regulation.

The conventional wisdom about the period of activism in the area of economic regulation is that for a long period, the Supreme Court was captured by a group of conservative ideologues who did indeed read. Herbert Spencer's *Social Statics* into the Constitution. This activism is seen by some as a long misguided attempt to, King Canute-like, tell the tides of history not to come in. And it is true that in the long run, this extended period of activism of the Court in the economic area did not succeed. Still, it lasted for several decades before it was undone.

Furthermore, although most might see it as an incidental consideration in analyzing this episode in our constitutional history, or certainly a debatable one, it is arguable that this century's story of the Supreme Court and economic regulation really involves *two* episodes of activism. The first is the commonly accepted one that has been discussed and examined here and elsewhere--the pre-1937 period. But the terms of the Settlement of 1937 are really activist as well, though they are not usually seen as such. That, of course, is because they involve a declaration by the Court that legislatures, and particularly the Congress, have authority now that could be described as plenary over economic regulation.

Because this grant involves renunciation by the Court of its previous assertion of activism and involves deference by the Court to the elected branches, it is seen by most as judicial restraint, not as judicial activism. But the deference disguises a kind of activism too since the constitutional doctrine that the Court then unambiguously set forth arguably involved a grant of power to Congress. Before 1937, few could have conscientiously argued that Congress's constitutional powers were clearly quite this unrestrained or that there were not some commercial transactions beyond its regulatory reach. It is not just deference to Congress and state legislatures, and the end of a misguided period of activism, that accounts for the success and longevity of the Settlement of 1937. It is arguable that the settlement itself is in part an example of successful judicial activism, and that it is this unambiguous grant of new constitutional authority to Congress too that has helped make this settlement last through the decades to today.

In any case, the question remains: how does the original controversial era of activism in the economic arena differ from the controversial era of civil liberties and civil rights activism that followed, or does it? Some would answer it does not, that in both eras the Supreme Court was equally wrong and wrong-headed; that in both eras a group of ideologues gained control of the Court and attempted to read their ideology into the Constitution. The only difference is that one group was conservative and the other group was liberal.

But under the "test" adopted for this book, the Warren Court's activism is "successful" because its fundamentals have lasted, while the original activism of the earlier era is "unsuccessful" because it did not. Of course, given that the first era did last for many decades, the answer might simply be that the first era was successful for so long because it did fit with its context in the broadest sense during a long period. And it ended after such a long time only when the basic underlying societal forces developed and shifted to the point where that activism and its accompanying doctrinal innovations no longer fit the context. Under a similar analysis, one might posit that the same fate will ultimately befall the major accomplishments of the Warren Court. That it simply has not happened yet does not mean it will not happen someday and perhaps, rather soon.

Yet there are some differences already apparent that suggest that the matter is not so simple. Unquestionably Substantive Due Process had an ideological component that reflected the social power of the rise of large industrial corporations and financial entities in the decades of this activism. Much of what is now seen as ideological excess was time-bound and something of the same can be said of the Warren Court.

But the Court in the first era was not uncompromisingly ideological. Even during the times of its most frequent and outrageous intervention, it would still sometimes allow economic regulation at both the state and federal levels to go forward. Despite the frequent outrageous outcomes, the major continuing offense of the activism in this era lay in the activism itself. The Court insisted that it would review the appropriateness of state and federal regulatory effort, sometimes approving, sometimes disapproving, leaving a patchwork of results and an endless uncertainly about what it would and would not permit.

It was actually in the early to mid-1800s, when Congress was essentially inactive in this area, that the Court first took on in a limited way the role of delinator and protector of national commerce and development.[29] Given congressional inaction, for the Court to have undertaken this activism at a time when commerce and development was still a minority interest in a primarily agrarian nation may arguably have been justified.

29. See *Gibbons v. Ogden*, 22 U.S. (9 Wheat.) 1 (1824); *Cooley v. Board of Wardens*, 53 U.S. (12 How.) 299 (1851).

But to have dramatically increased its activities in the late 1800s and into the twentieth century, when commerce and corporate industrial development became dominant in America, came to seem increasingly gratuitous and irrelevant. The doctrine pronounced was not any real contribution. It was primarily the incidental result of the Supreme Court arrogating to itself the right to say "yes" or "no" to particular regulatory thrusts.

On the other hand, the core of the major doctrinal innovations of the Warren Court survive today even though elements of the ideology that accompanied some of them may sometimes seem irrelevant and the ideology that has dominated the Court in recent years is a very different one. This suggests that the major decisions that marked Warren Court activism fit the long run American context in some deeper way, that they were not simply the imposition of an ideology or the assertion by the Court of a monitoring prerogative. Perhaps the major doctrinal innovations of the Warren Court will still be undone, but there is no real evidence that this will happen. Indeed, the reverse increasingly seems likely.

two/ The Success of Warren Court Activism

The great period of mid-century judicial activism primarily associated with the Warren Court, but which preceded it in part and continued for a time after Warren's departure from the Court, has been a success. This is true in the sense that the principal doctrinal accomplishments of the period have largely survived and become accepted as an integral part of modern America despite the continuing controversy that surrounds them. Though subjected to strenuous attack and vigorous efforts at judicial counterrevolution over two decades, the Warren Court revolution has persisted and prevailed in many of its most fundamental doctrinal aspects.

These accomplishments fall into two general categories: the advancement of equality and the nationalization civil liberties standards. They are interrelated achievements in that, at their core, they frequently involved the Court utilizing the Constitution to dismantle prevailing local and state arrangements, a matter explored more extensively in chapter six.

In the area of equality, the elimination of officially sanctioned racial discrimination is an accomplishment that must rank first. But notable too are the achievement of legislative reapportionment and the first recognition in the early 1970s by the Burger Court of limited constitutional protection against gender discrimination. The nationalization of civil liberty saw the effective incorporation of virtually all important guarantees of the Bill of Rights with particularly important doctrinal development that resulted in broad support for a libertarian conception of free speech.

Although Earl Warren was appointed in 1953 by President Eisenhower, the Warren Court did not reach what most see as its period of maximum activism until the mid-1960s brought a reliable five-man liberal majority. William Brennan, another Eisenhower appointee, joined the Court in the 1950s and, when added to Warren and to Justices William Douglas and Hugo Black from the Roosevelt era, produced a significant, but not always dominant, bloc of liberals. They were joined by Kennedy appointee Arthur Goldberg in the early 1960s who was himself replaced shortly thereafter by Johnson appointee Abe Fortas. Occasional defection from liberal predictability by Warren or Black meant less to liberal success with the addition of Thurgood Marshall under President Lyndon Johnson. At this point only John Harlan and Potter Stewart, Eisenhower appointees, and often Byron White, a Kennedy appointee, were reliable conservative votes.

Given that the Warren Court's liberal majority developed only gradually, the unanimity of *Brown v. Board of Education,*[1] which, in popular perception at least, dramatically opened the Warren Court era, was certainly not automatic. But the Warren era did begin with this historic achievement for the cause of equality, and equality continued to be both a central theme of Warren Court liberal activism over the next two decades and the principal focus of strong conservative criticism and objection.[2]

Among the other dimensions to Warren Court egalitarianism was the expansion of criminal procedure guarantees to the state and local levels. Though this was technically a matter of Bill of Rights incorporation, it should not be overlooked that a primary thrust of this activity was equalitarian. Since of the most criminally accused come from the least privileged portions of society, it is such people who are the prime beneficiaries of this doctrine. *Malloy v. Hogan*[3] incorporated the Fifth Amendment's guarantee against self-incrimination. *Mapp v. Ohio*[4] required state courts to exclude evidenc e obtained in violation of the Fourth Amendment's guarantee against unreasonable search and seizure. *Gideon v. Wainwright*[5] required that state courts provide an attorney for indigent defendants in all serious criminal cases.

These decisions culminated in *Miranda v. Arizona,*[6] which most dramatically illustrated the equalizing nature of these decisions. After all, the educated, the sophisticated, and the experienced will normally know of their right to remain silent and their right to have

---

1. 347 U.S. 483 (1954).
2. Mark Tushnet, ed., *The Warren Court in Historical and Political Perspective.* (Charlottesville: University Press of Virginia, 1993).
3. 378 U.S. 1 (1964).
4. 367 U.S. 643 (1961).
5. 372 U.S. 335 (1963).
6. 384 U.S. 436 (1966).

their lawyer present. It is those who lack these advantages who need to be warned and reminded of their rights.

The other major Warren Court thrust for equality in America is found in the reapportionment decisions.[7] When they came down, these decisions were not well received by significant portions of the academic community and the political establishment.[8] The rulings were attacked as simplistic, as imposing a rigid ideological egalitarianism on a subtle and complex Madisonian system. Many in politics who were threatened by reapportionment or closely associated with interests whose influence would be diminished organized a nearly successful effort to get a modifying constitutional amendment through Congress.

This remarkable effort was accompanied, however, by a deafening silence from the general public, whose reaction to the idea of "one man, one vote" was doubtless "good idea, thought we had that." The Court's activism prevailed because malapportionment was indefensible in the broad context of mid-twentieth-century American society and the remedy was comprehensive yet simple. In fact, malapportionment, unlike gerrymandering,[9] is easily and universally detectable and subject to an easy, clear-cut and universally understandable remedy.

The significance of reapportionment was real, but its effects were undoubtedly softened (and in that sense, perhaps, made more acceptable) because by the time it was broadly implemented, suburbanization had ameliorated the sharp urban-rural split that marked politics in many states in the first decades of the century. It was the developing moderate suburbs, not the declining cities, that were the primary beneficiaries of reapportionment. But here again, the heart of a major Warren Court activist thrust survives despite criticism.

---

7. See *Baker v. Carr*, 369 U.S. 186 (1962); *Reynolds v. Sims*, 377 U.S. 533 (1964); *Lucas v. 44th General Assembly*, 377 U.S. 713 (1964).

8. See Robert G. Dixon, Jr., *Democratic Representation* (New York: Oxford University Press, 1968).

9. Malapportionment involves districts of unequal population. Gerrymandering involves drawing district boundaries to take in or leave out certain voters to achieve a political end. The name comes from a district which after being redrawn by Massachusetts Governor Gerry, critics thought looked like a salamander. Districts may be apportioned equally but still be gerrymandered. The Court has recently set some limits on egregious gerrymandering involving districts of truly extreme shapes, but where districts lack outrageous shapes, it is extremely difficult to articulate a clear standard for prohibited gerrymandering that would permit consistent udicial enforcement.

Although Earl Warren is reported to have believed that the reapportionment decisions were the most important accomplishment of his period as Chief Justice, most observers doubtless would see *Brown* as the Warren Court's most historically significant decision and the struggle to end racial discrimination as the principal area of historic accomplishment. The Supreme Court's effective overruling of *Plessey v. Ferguson,*[10] by holding that separate but equal was inherently unequal, undermined the constitutional support for the rigidly entrenched racial caste system of the South.

Denial of rights to African-Americans has always been intimately involved with the peculiarities of the federal system and vindication of those rights with the expansion of national power. Racial segregation was originally ratified by the Supreme Court in *Plessey v. Ferguson* as part of a broad turning away by the national government and the national political community from concern for the then-recently freed southern Blacks. The case was one of several that involved the systematic gutting, through narrow judicial interpretation, of the national power conferred by the Reconstruction amendments. Observers have generally concluded that the Court of the post-Reconstruction period felt that an interpretation of the amendments that would broadly vindicate the rights of Blacks would permit an expansion of national authority so great as to threaten what was seen as an acceptable balance of power between the two levels of the federal system. Given this choice, they chose to protect the federal system. In the modern era, the undoing of *Plessey* through *Brown* and its progeny has involved the federal courts in what has undoubtedly been their most extensive and controversial exercise of authority at the expense of local power and sensibility.

The Court held that separate but equal was inherently unequal and required that dual school systems must be eliminated "with all deliberate speed."[11] But the *Brown* decision should be understood as fundamentally an expression of the unacceptability of official racism. At root, *Brown* has come to mean that the state may not be used by some elements of society to impose burdens on others because of their race. The use of state power by one group to isolate and stigmatize[12] another,

---

10. 163 U.S. 537 (1896).

11. *Brown v. Board of Education (II),* 349 U.S. 294 (1955).

12. Stigmatization suggests a "message." And Charles R. Lawrence III in his article "If He Hollers Let Him Go: Regulating Racist Speech on Campus," found as Chapter 3 in Mari Matsuda et al., *Words That Wound* (Boulder: Westview Press, 1993), argues that segregation was fundamentally a message that was forbidden by reinterpretation of the equal protection clause and that,

to institutionalize and make "official" practice those private prejudices that still persist in our diverse society, is to embark on a course of action so serious and threatening that it must be forbidden and all lingering effects of prior action eliminated.

Much has been made of the fact that the extensive levels of urban integration that the Supreme Court sanctioned and the lower federal courts struggled for have not been achieved in most places. Indeed, in recent times, demographic changes have produced historicly high levels of racial isolation in public schools, in some areas and current overall national trends are not promising. In the end, what was achieved during the Warren and post-Warren eras, in crude and inexact fashion, was a significant level of desegregation, particularly in the South, that made credible the Warren Court's original command to refrain from and eliminate the prior effects of official, government-authorized segregation. Certainly it was necessary and appropriate to eliminate officially sanctioned dual school systems and the segregation that was directly and reasonably traceable to it. It was arguably less appropriate for courts to seek to impose a level of integration that likely would not have existed had there never been officially sanctioned segregation.

Many of the decisive remedy cases came after the Warren Court had technically ended. *Swann v. Charlotte Mecklenberg*[13] in 1971, (about two years after the retirement of Earl Warren from the Court), which affirmed extensive busing remedies; *Millikan v. Bradley,*[14] which sharply limited metropolitan remedies; and *Keyes v. Denver,*[15] which held that establishment of unconstitutional official action in one part of a city school system created a presumption that the action

---

therefore, other messages that denigrate people on racial grounds may also be controlled under the authority of that clause. But all governmental action contains a message. It was the institutionalization of the message in the official requirement of segregated facilities and services that was outlawed so that the message was not just private prejudice, or even the expressed opinion of individual government members, but the message made manifest in the actual practice of government. The stigmatization does send a special message of inferiority, but the core of the stigma arises from the practice, not primarily from words associated with it. The message alone, left as words, was not forbidden. Today, individual principal government actors may still believe in segregation and they may even constitutionally express the opinion that racial segregation is a good thing, but they may not act officially to practice that belief.

13. 402 U.S. 1 (1971).
14. 418 U.S. 717 (1974).
15. 413 U.S. 189 (1973).

impacted the entire system, are among the most significant cases of the immediate post-Warren Court. *Keyes, Millikan,* and other cases that supported extensive affirmative remedies would have been decided the same way had Warren and those who left soon after him continued to serve and indeed, the 5-4 *Millikan* case undoubtedly would have gone the other way, opening the door for some compulsory metropolitan busing remedies. Thus, even where school desegregation remedies and doctrines were significantly developed after the end of the Warren Court, it is really not fundamentally wrong of critics to attribute them to that Court's activity. The equalitarian impulse so significantly developed by the Warren Court did set in motion several highly controversial processes of doctrinal development that continued well into the 1970s, albeit perhaps at a less accelerated pace.

This equalitarian impulse that was so much a part of the Warren Court did have an ideological component that became embodied in much remedy doctrine that continues to provoke sharp controversy. At a more fundamental level, the impulse grew out of historical and social developments and experiences that provided a deeper context for much of the Warren Court's work and accounts for the long-term survival of its basic accomplishments. American society had undergone enormous social changes between the time of *Plessey* and the time of *Brown*. These social changes ultimately produced political changes, and these in turn were ultimately reflected on the Court. After all, the doctrinal possibilities that led to *Brown* were always there; the Harlan dissent in *Plessey* proves that. Harlan said, "in view of the Constitution, in the eye of the law, there is no superior, dominant ruling class of citizens. There is no caste here. Our Constitution is color blind and neither knows nor tolerates classes among citizens." It was the broader social changes that opened the way for this doctrinal approach to receive a receptive and, indeed, a supportive audience from the Court in the 1950s, 1960s, and early 1970s.

The immigration from southern and eastern Europe of the "new-stock" Americans, primarily Catholic and Jewish, was one important change. The immigrants seemed very different to many "old-stock" Americans, who were primarily Protestant from northern and western Europe, and much of "old-stock" America supported limitation of this immigration though passage of restrictive legislation. In many places and situations, much of "old stock" America also practiced social and employment discrimination against "new-stock" America.

Important too was the internal migration of large numbers of African-Americans from the South to the North in the first several decades of the century. African-Americans could vote in northern cities, something they could not do in the rural South of the early twentieth century. Gradually, the new-stock Americans came to vote in large numbers in northern cities too, and over time, there developed a political constituency for what might be called the civil rights idea: the concept that an individual should have access to rights and opportunities without regard to race, creed, color, or national origin. The idea included the proposition that government should act to ensure that these rights and opportunities were actually made available on a nondiscriminatory basis. In much of the country it became possible to win office in state legislatures and Congress running on a pledge to enact this idea into law.

In 1948 the Democratic Convention adopted a civil rights plank prompting a Southern walkout and a third party presidential race by Strom Thurmond. Civil rights bills began to make their way through Congress, though not by a majority large enough to overcome Southern filibusters. The armed forces were desegregated, and the Supreme Court began to crack down on "separate but equal."

In 1938 in *Missouri ex rel. Gaines v. Canada,*[16] the Court held that separate but equal was not satisfied by a state's offer to pay tuition for a qualified Black resident to a law school in another state; it required that equal facilities be provided within the state. In *Sweat v. Painter,*[17] the separate law schools operated by Texas for Black and White students were held not equal in light of the inferior educational opportunities and facilities provided in the Black law school.In *McLaurin v. Oklahoma,*[18] admitting Black students but separating them within the school was stuck down. Internal segregation limited student interaction, and the Court's recognition that such interaction was a part of the educational process seriously undermined what remained of "separate but equal." Therefore, *Brown* did not come as any real surprise to those who were paying close attention.

The *Brown* decision held that separate but equal was inherently unequal and violated the equal protection clause. But Warren's opinion concerned itself with a number of matters that some have criticized. For example, the opinion refers to psychological tests administered by Dr. Kenneth Clark to Black children in segregated schools utilizing Black and White dolls and his conclusions that these tests illustrate the feelings of inferiority he found in segregated Black children.[19] The

16. 305 U.S. 337 (1938).

17. 339 U.S. 629 (1950).

18. 339 U.S. 637 (1950).

19. "Indeed, many legal scholars believe that a finding of psychological harm was not necessary for the option and that the adequacy of social science

decision also speaks of public school resources and equal educational opportunity and the relationship between these, which has been much discussed in subsequent years. Over time, school desegregation developed into a complex phenomenon debated continuously on the educational, philosophical, psychological, political, and legal levels.

But again, what *Brown* was about at the deepest level was Jim Crow, the comprehensive system of official practice that dominated the South and the fact that enforced racial separation was a profound form of institutionally stigmatizing one race as officially inferior. The first Justice Harlan had it right in his dissent to *Plessy* when he said that the Constitution is color-blind, and it would have actually been sufficient in *Brown* just to have said that. *Brown* must come out the same even if Clark's tests of children attending segregated schools had found anger, or resentment, or even some kind of defiant pride.

Jews and others placed in Nazi death camps for "racial" reasons during World War II may or may not have developed feelings of inferiority as a result of the Nazi state's systematic and "logical" policy of official stigmatization leading to separation, then to dehumanization, and finally, extermination. Their subjective feelings about such treatment are ultimately beside the point. It is the objective consequences of such official state policies carried to their logical conclusions that overwhelm in their impact. That is why the Constitution must prohibit them.

The justices of the *Brown* Court, like all Americans of their time period, had this lesson brought home to them in the shocking news-films and firsthand reports that accompanied the liberation of Europe just a few short years before. Had this lesson been more clearly and emphatically stressed in the decision, and the deepest reason for Brown been kept firmly in view in the ensuing years, some of the less productive aspects of remedy fights might have been avoided.

Perhaps in retrospect, some aspects of the Warren Court's egalitarianism do seem too "easy." They were premised on liberal

---

evidence cited is not an important consideration. . . Moreover, the most important of Brown's declarations--that separate facilities are *inherently* unequal--can be viewed as a prima facie declaration that does not require demonstration of harm or negative effects. Something that is inherently unequal by definition violates the equal protection clause of the Fourteenth Amendment." David Armor, *Forced Justice: School Desegregation and the Law* (New York: Oxford University Press, 1995), 21 citing Mark G. Yudof, "School Desegregation: Legal Realism, Reasoned Elaboration, and Social Science Research in the Supreme Court," *Law and Contemporary Problems* 42 (1978): 57-109.

assumptions of the 1940s, 1950s, and 1960s that even many liberals have come to question: a sense of the inevitability of progress; an expectation of seemingly endless wealth that would be easily produced from a technological cornucopia; and a confidence in a great potential for positive "social engineering" through the application of scientific rationalism and money to difficult social problems.

This egalitarianism was also easy in that it opposed itself to a bigotry so enormous and clear-cut that the word "evil" properly applies without exaggeration. One need not be a conservative to appreciate that many of today's equality issues are complex and subtle, and that constitutionalizing them, and most particularly their remediation, is often of dubious practical wisdom even where motivated by admirable instincts.

It may be that the parts of *Brown* that have been most criticized, the implicit faith in social science, particularly when used in support of liberal values, and the concern with subjective psychological sensitivity, not to mention the somewhat rigid education-school social engineering sensibility that informed many of the subsequent equitable remedies, are all, at least in part, products of their time period. Some critics have found them naive, or simplistic, or even a bit patronizing. But the core of *Brown* grew out of the real and overwhelming experience of World War II and the light it shed on the harsh realities of American history over decades and even centuries.

That this was *Brown's* underlying meaning has been at some level broadly understood in America even if not always clearly articulated. Although there is obviously still much racism in America, the cruder forms of official racism are now almost nowhere sanctioned. While this situation is radically inadequate to the contemporary societal need, it remains a remarkable societal accomplishment. A great part of this accomplishment has ultimately flowed from the broad thrust of Warren Court equal protection jurisprudence; this too is something that is widely understood.[20]

---

20. Gerald N. Rosenberg in *The Hollow Hope* (Chicago: University of Chicago Press, 1991) argues that the role of the *Brown* decision itself was minor in achieving ultimate social change, and that the successes of the Civil Rights Movement of the 1960s are primarily attributable to underlying societal developments and trends. Rosenberg creates something of a straw man in his "Dynamic Court model," which he successfully demolishes; few people believe that *Brown* alone brought change "on the ground" or that the Court acting alone can normally produce immediate and significant social change. Even if Warren Court equal protection jurisprudence took years to play out, and even if it did require all kinds of other political and social changes to have real

What was accomplished is so truly significant that it transcends any arguable time-bound deficiencies and this significance is now widely appreciated. Many, perhaps most, White Southerners now realize that ending official segregation liberated them as much (or almost as much) as it liberated African-Americans. Many conservatives who still criticize Warren Court activism struggle to make an exception for *Brown*. But of course, *Brown* was not an exception; it was central to an understanding of the Warren Court, its accomplishment, and its activism.

Warren Court egalitarianism did stretch basic doctrine quite far in some particular cases. For example, *Reitman v. Mulkey*[21] seemed to suggest that once the state broke new ground in anti-discrimination law, even where there was no obligation to do so, it was "stuck" with that policy and could not reverse itself.*Katzenbach v. Morgan*[22] seemed to suggest that Congress might have the power to define and expand constitutional rights. Taken together with *South Carolina v. Katzenbach*,[23] the Court was seen as granting Congress extremely broad powers to enforce the Fifteenth and Fourteenth Amendments. The potential in these latter decisions seemed great indeed including the effective eradication of the lines separating private action from state action.[24]

Occasionally, some cases did give hints of doctrinal potential for notions of economic equality, which made many conservatives quite nervous.[25] The *Griffen v. Illinois*[26] majority was accused by Justice Harlan in dissent with holding that equal protection required of the government "an affirmative duty to lift the handicaps flowing from

---

impact, and even if one accepts the complete validity of Rosenberg's examination of the evidence that leads him to conclude that leading actors in these other developments were not much motivated by Brown, this still does not lead to the ultimate conclusion that Brown was unimportant. Interestingly, despite its different specific objectives, the ultimate effect of the Rosenberg book is to more firmly support the thesis of this book: that the major doctrinal thrusts of Warren Court era activism reflected deep societal change and survived for that reason.

21. 387 U.S. 369 (1967).

22. 384 U.S. 641 (1966).

23. 383 U.S. 301 (1966).

24. See Archibald Cox "Foreword: Constitutional Adjudication and the Promotion of Human Rights," *Harvard Law Review* 80 (1966), 91.

25. Of course the same cases pleased and excited some progressives. See Michelman, "Foreword: On Protecting the Poor Through the 14th Amendment," *Harvard Law Review* 83 (1969), 7.

26. 351 U.S. 12 (1956).

differences in economic circumstances." The approach was expanded in *Douglas v. California*.[27] These cases required that transcripts and counsel be provided for criminal appeals by indigents. Then in *Shapiro v. Thompson*,[28] a Warren Court majority, not including Justices Warren or Black, struck down state and District of Columbia residency requirements conditioning receipt of welfare assistance upon at least one year's residence prior to application.

Cases like these, though occasional, were inevitably controversial, attacked as manifestations of the "liberal ideology" of the times. To many critics they still symbolize a period of judicial activism that seemed to some to have been marked by a willingness to stretch doctrine too far, too easily to achieve liberal objectives. But whatever the merits of particular criticisms of cases like these, it seems fair to say that while such cases are unquestionably reflective of the spirit of the Warren Court, they do not constitute the dominant parts of its work. The major doctrinal innovations of the Warren Court that, taken together, made America a far more equal place, do transcend the ideology of their time of origin, and thus they survive today in Supreme Court constitutional interpretation even though the ideology that originally infused them no longer dominates the Court.

After equality, the other major areas of Warren Court activism are largely subsumed under the heading of "incorporating of the Bill of Rights through the due process clause of the Fourteenth Amendment." This process of imposing the Bill of Rights upon states and localities dramatically expanded prior understanding of several basic guarantees, both as a practical matter and from the standpoint of doctrinal development.

Many Americans still do not realize that there was a time when the Bill of Rights did not bind state and local governments, and that this meant that if these governments violated civil liberties, no remedy was available from the Supreme Court.[29] Not until this century did the Court began to take seriously the idea that the enactment of the Fourteenth Amendment had altered this situation.

The Warren Court did not initiate incorporation of the Bill of Rights through the due process clause of the Fourteenth Amendment, but in a number of major decisions it dramatically expanded and developed the process of incorporation and took it to a point where it is

27. 372 U.S. 353 (1963).

28. 394 U.S. 618 (1969).

29. See *Barron v. Baltimore*, 32 U.S. (7 Pet.) 243 (1833).

no exaggeration to say that the Warren Court set national standards for civil liberties in America.

There were several principal areas in which the Warren Court was active. In the area of free speech and press, the record is complex but the accomplishment significant. The Warren Court began in the wake of the McCarthy era with its prosecutions of Communist leaders under the Smith Act for conspiring to overthrow the government of the United States. In its first few years, the Court cut away at Smith Act prosecutions in several decisions, which signaled a more libertarian approach. Yet it never went the whole distance and directly confronted the tension between the administration of the act and the First Amendment, but upheld several dubious prosecutions even as it announced liberalizing technical doctrines that ultimately made further prosecutions impractical.

Arguably, its most significant doctrinal achievement in the area of speech and press was in *New York Times v. Sullivan*.[30] The case arose out of the civil rights struggle in the South. The civil rights movement depended heavily on media coverage and perhaps could not have succeeded if the media intimidation that such libel cases involved had been allowed to stand. The decision, which drastically limits the ability of public figures to sue for libel, significantly echoed the views of Alexander Meiklejohn, who had argued in his writings that in a democracy, the people were the ultimate governors and all speech made by them in that capacity was absolutely privileged.

Of courses, the decision does not go that far since it does allows libel actions upon a showing of actual malice or reckless disregard of the truth, and as time has passed, these "exceptions" have not been without problems and controversy. But *Sullivan* is nonetheless a sweeping decision emphasizing a developing perspective on First Amendment doctrine that has its roots in the original resistance to the Sedition Act of 1798.[31]

Edwards v. South Carolina[32] and related cases greatly increased the obligation upon public authorities to defend speakers and demonstrators facing potentially hostile crowds. Although justices writing on both sides of *Edwards* distinguished the case from *Feiner v.*

---

30. 376 U.S. 254 (1971).

31. In the process of announcing the decision, the Court took the unusual step of declaring the Sedition Act of 1798 unconstitutional over 160 years after its enactment. See Anthony Lewis, *Make No Law: The Sullivan Case and the First Amendment* (New York: Random House, 1991).

32. 372 U.S. 299 (1963).

New York, [33] the case in fact struck a balance much more weighted toward free speech than *Feiner*. It is very significant that both *Sullivan* and *Edwards,* which broke significant new ground in First Amendment doctrine, grew out of the Civil Rights struggle in the South.

In *Brandenburg v. Ohio*[34] in 1969 the Court avoided use of the words "clear and present danger," doubtless because of the many prior times they had been used but their literal meaning not followed.[35] Still, the standard applied in *Brandenburg* to advocacy of the use of force or of law violation--that "such advocacy is directed to inciting or producing imminent lawless action and is likely to incite or produce such action"--is in fact the clear and present danger test, strictly and forcefully applied at last.

These cases from the Warren Court initiated a process of fundamental doctrinal change, much of which bore fruit after Chief Justice Warren had left the Court and thus, the Warren Court had technically come to an end. Notable in 1971 is the overturning of the conviction in *Cohen v. California*[36] of a man who walked through a courthouse with "Fuck the Draft" written on his jacket. A Court majority lead by Justice Harlan refused to sanction the suppression of offensive speech that did not fit within one of the recognized exceptions to the First Amendment. Since Cohen's statement was not obscene, did not present a clear and present danger, and did not constitute fighting words, the First Amendment protected it given that "one man's vulgarity is another man's lyric."

These speech and press decisions and the doctrine they represent involve significant developments. The truth is that although much liberal opinion advocated basic libertarian notions of speech toleration in the 1950s and early 1960s, perhaps largely as a result of the unhappy experience of the McCarthy era, the same cannot really be said of the preponderance of conservative opinion of that period.

Today, basic doctrines of speech tolerance are widely accepted on both sides of the spectrum. The *Hustler* cartoon case[37] and the closely

---

33. 340 U.S. 315 (1951).

34. 395 U.S. 444 (1969).

35. The phrase was first used by Justice Oliver Wendell Holmes in *Schenck v. United States,* 249 U.S. 47 (1919). Yet by any rational standard, the actions of Schenck failed to present a danger that was either clear or present. They offered nothing like Holmes's famous hypothetical of falsely shouting fire in a crowed theater.

36. 403 U.S. 15 (1971).

37. *Hustler Magazine v. Fallwell,* 485 U.S. 46 (1988). The continuing dominance of libertarian speech views on the Court can be seen in recent

decided flag burning cases[38] are perhaps the clearest contemporary illustrations of this fact. The *Hustler* case was unanimous, the decision written by Chief Justice Rehnquist holding that no recovery for emotional distress by Reverend Jerry Falwell could be had against Hustler magazine for publishing a cartoon parody depicting Falwell as engaging in incest with his mother behind an outhouse. The flag salute cases sharply divided the Court, but justices widely identified as strong liberals and strong conservatives could be found on both sides.

That the tolerant libertarian view of the free speech clause has such broad support in contemporary America and on a Court that has become increasingly conservative is yet another example of Warren Court activism moving doctrine in a direction that has both persisted and further developed.[39] The end result, a broad acceptance of this tolerant libertarian view of free speech, is an accomplishment that arguably ranks with the ending of official racism in scope and importance though it is far less widely appreciated or understood. That there remain new and significant contemporary challenges to free speech in America from both sides of the political spectrum does not detract from the fundamental importance of this achievement.[40]

Here again the core of Warren Court accomplishment, this time in the area of speech, grew out of experiences that both changed the society and in turn reflected basic societal change, giving truth both to Justice Holmes's famous saying about experience being the life of the law, and to this book's thesis that activism succeeds if it fits the fundamentals of a changing societal context. The civil rights movement of the 1960s both dramatized the need for broad speech doctrine and provided the occasion for its expansion and development. Influential too were the protests of the Vietnam War, which were not always peaceful or limited to speech. *Cohen v. California* can be understood as saying, among other things, that it is better to allow strong, full speech expression that shows contempt and hostility for the draft than to

---

cases like *Reno v. A.C.L.U.*, 117 S.Ct. 2329 (1997), where the Court struck down the Communications Decency Act.

38. *Texas v. Johnson*, 491 U.S. 397 (1989); *United States v. Eichman*, 110 S.Ct. 2404 (1990).

39. For an interesting exploration of why we tolerate speech we hate, see Lee Bollinger, *The Tolerant Society* (New York: Oxford University Press, 1986). Conservative attitudes toward protecting hate speech were demonstrated in *R.A.V. v. City of St. Paul*, 112 S.Ct. 2538 (1992).

40. See for example, Nat Hentoff, *Free Speech for Me--But Not for Thee* (New York: HarperCollins Publishers, 1992).

have young people taking over buildings, or breaking into draft boards and destroying files.

Perhaps one additional reason why the conservative movement that come to power in the 1980s contained elements which so strongly respected libertarian speech is that the ascendency was preceded by a self-conscious effort to make conservatism a movement of ideas. Certainly a growing conservative intellectual establishment saw itself as having challenged the liberal intellectual establishment that had dominated in previous decades and conservatism as having finally succeeded because of the force of its ideas.

Whether conservatism really came to power in America because of its ideas is debatable, but that it was accompanied by a sizable intellectual establishment that had used free speech vigorously and had an interest in its preservation is not. Some would also argue that in recent years conservative interest in free speech has been stimulated by the phenomena that has come to be known as "political correctness"--a movement on many university campuses associated with the academic left that is perceived as advocating restriction of established libertarian speech protections in pursuit of equality interests and group sensibilities.[41]

More weighted with ambiguity is the argument that conservative support for libertarian free speech doctrine comes with a high price--that of blocking government efforts to limit the impact of large aggregates of wealth and property upon the political and electoral process.[42] Supreme Court decisions have placed what many see as excessive restrictions on the ability of Congress and state legislatures to limit the amount of money that can be spent to influence the outcome of elections and referenda. Many believe that moderate regulation coupled with public financing is necessary to prevent large amounts of special interest money from controlling the process and that the Supreme Court's use of the First Amendment to block these efforts is a kind of backdoor *Lochner*.

Unless and until the Court sustains restrictions designed to limit the ability of money to influence elections (or the Constitution is explicitly amended to permit such limitations), we will be unable to determine if the contemporary willingness of conservatives to join with liberals in supporting libertarian speech concepts in cases like *Hustler* or the flag burning cases is contingent on Court vindication of all of the free speech

---

41. See Paul Berman, ed., *Debating PC* (New York: Dell Books, 1992).

42. For a discussion of what is described as a New Deal for speech doctrine, see Cass Sunstein, *Democracy and the Problem of Free Speech* (New York: Free Press, 1993) particularly chapters 2, 3, and 4.

claims of wealth. There is no reason to automatically assume this is true.[43] All one can say with certainty is that today there seems to be a serious commitment to libertarian ideas of free speech across a broader spectrum of intellectual opinion than America has ever seen.[44]

Warren Court doctrine in the other major First Amendment area, that marked by the complementary clauses guaranteeing free exercise of religion and prohibiting establishment of religion, has also been surrounded by controversy. The meaning of separation of church and state involves distinctions that are often subtle and difficult. In the modern era, formal discrimination by government against well-known sects has become virtually nonexistent. Increasingly, socially established religious opinion, which usually dominates government, has been inclined to mutual toleration, but is often unwilling to extend the same equal status to less traditional views or to views that are seen as irreligious.

The Warren Court's doctrinal innovation in the area of church and state had at least three notable aspects. The free exercise guarantee was interpreted on significant occasions to define religion very broadly so that belief in a supreme being could not be required; as a result, views not seen as really religious by the more conventional were given implicit legitimacy.[45] The Court also moved to give minority religious practice that conflicted with majority governmental policy greater degrees of exemption.[46] In its leading and most controversial doctrinal innovation, the Warren Court banned school prayer, announcing doctrine with both establishment and free exercise components.[47]

The common thread in these cases then, is the increased sensitivity and deference shown to views and practices that then were out of the

---

43. We do not assume that the libertarianism of liberals is contingent on maintaining the consumerism advantaged by cases like *Virginia Board of Pharmacy v. Virgina Consumer Council,* 425 U.S. 748 (1976).

44. On the importance of libertarian speech principles for the determination of knowledge see Jonathan Rauch, *Kindly Inquisitors* (Chicago: University of Chicago Press, 1993). The argument that *There's No Such Thing as Free speech . . . and It's a Good Thing Too!* is made by Stanley Fish in the book of that name (New York: Oxford University Press, 1994). Fish's claim that all phenomena are politicized and free speech neutrality unachievable is less significant or insightful than he seems to think. The fact that the ideal is rarely, indeed perhaps never, achieved in the real world does not establish that we would be better off operating without it.

45. See *U.S. v. Seeger,* 380 U.S. 163 (1965).

46. See *Sherbert v. Verner,* 374 U.S. 398 (1963).

47. *Engel v. Vitale,* 370 U.S. 421 (1962).

mainstream, either because they were not seen by traditionalists as religious at all or because, as minority religious sensibility or practices, they conflicted with majority-shaped governmental policy. It was the increasing diversity of America and the social and political "arrival" of minority ethnic and religious groups at midcentury that provided the context for this increased sensitivity and for the development of new doctrine.

In the leading school prayer case of *Engel v. Vitale,* a small number of parents of school children in New York challenged the state requirement that all public schools cause a brief prayer that the state board of regents had written to be said aloud in each class every day. The board believed that the prayer, which presupposed a God upon whom we depend, was nonsectarian, but the parents, identified in the case as Jewish, Unitarian, and agnostic, disagreed. After the decision came down, some clearly identifiable segments of the clergy supported it while others opposed it. The case demonstrates that there are points of view held by individuals and groups that claim protection under the religion clauses while simultaneously rejecting the most traditional views of what constitutes religion, and the Court recognized the legitimacy of these points of view.

The Supreme Court ruled in *Engel* that the prayer requirement was not saved by an adjustment that provided that any child who so desired could get up and leave the room when the prayer was recited. The Court held that the state could not put a child to the choice of staying for a prayer that offended his or her religious beliefs or leaving and subjecting him- or herself to the embarrassment that such an act would involve. More fundamentally, however, the Court's decisions in the area of school prayer seem to turn on the use of the state's authority to impose, sponsor, and conduct an exercise associated with a particular view of what constitutes religion in a sensitive educational environment where children are sent to take in and learn what the school authorities convey to them. It is fair to assume that if a group of atheists seized control of a school board and ordered teachers to require recitation of an "anti-prayer" each morning, the Court would find this equally unconstitutional. However, the unlikelihood of atheist takeovers actually happening doubtless means that the probability of Court parallelism in such an instance provides little solace to proponents of traditional religious views who support school prayer.

Attempts by authorities to provide for voluntary prayer in the schools highlight the situation. Truly voluntary prayer would be permissible in the public schools; indeed, it presumably could not be excluded unless it were disruptive. If a high school student were to pray quietly to him- or herself while walking in the hall between classes, it should be permissible. If a group of children voluntarily congregate for a brief prayer in one corner of the playground during recess, the Constitution presumably would not stand in their way. The controversy continues because these things, of course, do not often happen. Normally, young children will not pray without instruction from adult authority, and while the children are in school (compulsorily), the Court will not permit the public authority that supervises them to engage in the sponsorship of religious exercises.[48]

Admittedly, recent Court decisions have further softened or undercut some elements of established church-state doctrine[49] and other significant doctrinal changes remain possible. Still, as of this writing, most major doctrinal elements developed by the Warren Court (and its predecessor and successor Courts) still stand and overall, have shown remarkable staying power.

The activism associated with the Warren Court has been the center of concern to conservatives and the object of some defensiveness among liberals. Yet many of the greatest accomplishments of that Court remain broadly accepted and unchallenged. The destruction of legal racial segregation is unchallenged. The acceptance by large segments of American conservatism of much modern free speech doctrine is a major accomplishment. Although softened around the edges, the basics of Warren Court reapportionment doctrine still hold. While under attack, the core of Warren Court church-state doctrine still stands.[50] And even

---

48. A related church-state controversy was state aid to parochial schools. Modern doctrine on this issue began with *Everson v. Board of Education* 330 U.S. 1 (1947). There the Court endorsed Jefferson's wall of separation between church and State" as general doctrine, even as it approved the expenditure of public money for the transportation of school children to parochial schools under what came to be known as the child-benefit theory. The Warren Court continued an approach that held off major state aid to education while permitting some forms of indirect aid, though in some respects the Warren Court showed more flexibility on this issue than the subsequent Burger Court. Compare *Board of Regents v. Allen*, 392 U.S. 236 (1968) with *Lemon v. Kurtzman*, 403 U.S. 602 (1971).

49. *Lynch v. Donnelly*, 465 U.S. 668 (1984); *County of Allegheny v. American Civil Liberties Union*, 109 S.Ct. 3086 (1989).

50. It is notable though that in 1990 the Court's decision by Justice Scalia, in *Department of Human Resources of Oregon v. Smith*, 494 U.S. 884, denied free exercise protection for peyote use in Navaho religious rituals in the face of general legal prohibition. The decison was severely criticized by the three dissenting justices as overturning "a settled and inviolate principle of the[e] Court's First Amendment jurisprudence." Congress attempted to restore the

though Warren Court criminal procedure decisions and obscenity doctrine have been eroded in many respects, change in social and institutional practice has been so profound that the impact of doctrinal reversal has been limited. The reason for this is to be found in the broad emerging societal context within which the Warren Court operated, and the fit between this developing context and much of the doctrine that the Court promulgated over time.

The developing context extended beyond the temporal boundaries of the Warren Court, which technically ended with Warren's retirement in 1969. But it has now become commonplace to observe that the successor Burger Court, in the words of one commentator, was the "counterrevolution that wasn't."[51] President Richard M. Nixon ran for office in 1968 on a platform that included a promise to appoint "strict constructionists" to the Supreme Court. By this, it became clear, he meant judges who would not be activist and liberal, but conservative and restrained in the exercise of their power.

Personnel changes came quickly. The attempt by Warren to resign while President Johnson could still appoint his successor was thwarted by a Republican filibuster, and Nixon appointed the new chief justice, Warren Burger. Retirements, both natural and pressured, were sufficient in number that by the end of the Nixon-Ford administrations' eight years, five seats, a majority, had turned over and five new justices were appointed.

The struggle was often marked by partisanship and bitterness. In addition to the conflict over the chief justiceship mentioned above, the process of turnover had included the forcing out of Justice Fortas and the rejection by the Senate of two of President Nixon's appointees. But the five new appointments ultimately all had been made by two conservative Republican presidents well aware of the issues involved. (President Ford, when a congressional leader, had led unsuccessful attempts to impeach liberal Justice William O. Douglas.)

The personnel changes were not without some significant effect. Certainly there are decisions the Burger Court made that one may

---

doctrinal status quo ante by passing the Religious Restoration Act but a Court majority struck down the act in *City of Boerne v. Flores*, 117 S.Ct. 2157 (1997).

51. Vincent Blasi, ed., *The Burger Court: The Counter-Revolution that Wasn't*, (New York: Yale University Press, 1983). And T. Hensley, C. Smith and J. Baugh in *The Changing Supreme Court* (St. Paul: West Publishing Co., 1997) state: "our analyses lead to the conclusion that the Burger Court was substantially more conservative than the Warren Court but that the Burger Court justices did not substantially alter most of the leading precedents and doctrines of the Warren Court era." xxix.

reasonably assume would have come out differently if the Warren Court had continued. But, as discussed, in some important respects the early years of the Burger Court saw the further development of major doctrinal trends that began in earnest under the Warren Court. There were also some important decisions of the Burger Court that broke new activist constitutional ground in a direction that must be described as liberal. Considering its record as a whole, the Burger Court was more a matter of "lightening the foot on the accelerator" than "throwing the vehicle into reverse."

The Rehnquist Court has been another matter. In the 1980s the appointments of Antonin Scalia, Clarence Thomas, David Souter, Sandra Day O'Connor, and Anthony Kennedy, taken together, moved the Court further to the right, and few would deny that the tone and results were consistently different from its predecessors. Still, even after the passage of two decades marked by intense and sustained attempts to alter the Court through conservative appointments, it is not the erosion of Warren Court doctrine that is the significant story. Arguably, what is truly remarkable is the extent to which the broad outlines of most of the Warren Court revolution remain. (With the arrival of the Clinton administration, this period of deliberate conservative appointments has come to an end.)

There are many examples where the Burger Court decided cases differently than the Warren Court likely would have. Many, though not all, are a refusal to expand doctrine rather than its reversal. For example, in *Millikan v. Bradley*,[52] the Burger Court, by 5-4 margin, refused to sanction metropolitan school desegregation busing remedies involving compulsory suburban participation absent evidence of direct involvement by the suburban governments themselves. In *Moose Lodge v. Irvis*[53] another 5-4 majority refused to find state action sufficient to implicate the command of the equal protection clause in the providing of one of only a limited number of state licenses allowing the sale of liquor to a "private" Moose Lodge that declined to serve an African-American.

The issue of obscenity is a particularly dramatic example of a different approach. In this notable instance, Warren Court doctrine was purposefully overturned by its successor, the Burger Court. The Warren Court had radically liberalized the standards to be applied in obscenity cases. It dealt initially with obscenity in *Roth v. United*

52. 418 U.S. 717 (1974).
53. 407 U.S. 163 (1972).

States.[54] The Court first held that obscenity was not speech and not protected by the First Amendment, thus carving out a major exception to the free speech guarantee. A three point test was offered to determine what was obscene.

The test was revised in *Cleland's Memoirs of a Woman of Pleasure v. Attorney General of Massachusetts*.[55] That state had acted to ban the book, but the Court reversed with a statement of the test that made it very hard to ban any book successfully for many years thereafter. Under the *Cleland's Memoirs* test, for material to be obscene, it must be shown that: (1) the dominant theme of the material, taken as a whole, appeals to a prurient interest in sex; (2) the material is patently offensive because it affronts contemporary community standards relating to the description or representation of sexual matters; and (3) the material is utterly without redeeming social value.

In subsequent decisions the Court made it clear that the community whose standards must be affronted was the national community. This requirement was such that successful prosecution was normally impossible if the defendant had the resources to appeal to higher courts. Higher courts were likely to take a broad view of what the national community standards could tolerate and find some kind of redeeming social value in the material under attack.

Still, obscenity prosecutions were upheld in some circumstances. In *Ginzburg v. United States*[56] the Court, without actually reviewing the content of the publication in question, found that the advertising for it constituted "pandering." In effect, the Court said that if a publisher suggests in its advertising that it is selling obscene materials, we may take it at its word. And in *Ginsberg v. New York*[57] the Court upheld a statute that restricted the sale to minors of sexually explicit material that probably would not have failed the obscenity test when applied to an audience of adults.

These two case were exceptional in that the Court permitted prosecution of material in both that was probably not intrinsically obscene under the Court's then prevailing three point test. *Stanley v.*

---

54. 354 U.S. 476 (1957).

55. 383 U.S. 413 (1966).

56. 383 U.S. 463 (1966). It may not have helped the cause of *Eros* magazine publisher Ralph Ginzburg that he took out ads in major newspapers for his new venture suggesting that thanks to the U.S. Supreme Court, he would be carrying erotica to new limits. Ginzburg gave his magazine a hard cover and a hefty price, intending it for coffee tables. By today's standards, the actual magazine seems incredibly tame and innocuous.

57. 390 U.S. 629 (1968).

Georgia[58] was a different kind of exception; the materials involved probably were legally obscene, but the Court held that since Stanley had simply kept them in the privacy of his own home, he could not be arrested for possessing them.

Some observers concluded in the late 1960s that these three exceptional cases pointed the way to a final liberalization of obscenity standards that would permit adult private use of, and low-key commerce in, sexually explicit materials, whether obscene or not, but simultaneously permit strict regulation of public display and advertising of such material and of its sale to minors. The Court was known to be unhappy about being in the obscenity business; that is, many justices did not want to have to devote time to deciding whether particular books or movies were legally obscene.

A new Court position did emerge in 1973 under the Burger Court, but it was not the position these observers anticipated. The Court attempted to respond to criticism that the Supreme Court had loosed a tide of filth upon the country with a clear turn toward a new standard that the majority believed would improve the chance for successful obscenity prosecution.

The *Cleland's Memoirs* requirement that material be utterly without redeeming social value to be suppressed as obscene was seen as a standard virtually impossible to meet. Having the national, not the local, community as the standard in determining obscenity was seen as imposing what would be tolerable in Las Vegas or New York City upon Iowa or Mississippi.

With *Miller v. California*[59] the Burger Court announced a test that changed both of these. It substituted local community standards for those of the national community, and substituted for the requirement of lacking "redeeming social value" a new requirement that material that was otherwise unprotected had to possess "serious literary, artistic, political, or scientific, value" to gain First Amendment protection. Yet these changes had very limited practical results in light of American society's dramatic shift in its attitudes about sexuality in the early 1970s. Thus the Burger Court's efforts at reversal had only minimal immediate impact given the change in the broader societal context.[60] Even today, as sexual mores begin to feel the impact of the AIDS

58. 394 U.S. 557 (1969).

59. 413 U.S. 15 (1973).

60. Indeed, according to novelist John Updike, something of an expert in the matter, the Ford administration was the "high point" (if that is the correct phrase) of the post-war sexual revolution. See John Updike, *Memoirs of the Ford Administration* (New York: Knopf-Random House, 1992).

threat, sexually explicit material remains both available and controversial. *Miller v. California* and related cases may have altered the *Roth* and *Cleland's Memoirs* tests, but they could not reverse the broad cultural change encompassed by the sexual revolution of the 1960s and 1970s. The substance of American community standards has changed so radically in thirty years that successful prosecution is frequently difficult regardless of whether the community is national or local.

More recent developments in the societal context may yet finally sustain the Burger Court's attempt at reversal or at least encourage further doctrinal development permitting a more restrictive approach. At the same time, there are new currents in the debate today that suggest the possibility of even more significant change. The rise in the social and economic position of women is creating attention to the nature of pornography, questions about its commercialization, and argument over its contribution, if any, to the societal degradation of women and to violence against women.[61] Concern over violence in general, particularly on television, may highlight again the peculiar anomaly that American constitutional law permits, under certain circumstances, the prosecution of the excessively erotic, even though nonviolent, but not of the excessively violent if it is not erotic.

Warren Court doctrine in this controversial area developed in a historical context where "sophisticated" opinion reacted to the experiences of prior decades where literary masterpieces were banned, and "Comstockery" sought to suppress sexuality almost everywhere. In today's somewhat more complex context, further doctrinal evolution would not be surprising.

The area of criminal procedure doctrine presents a like situation. The development of doctrine surrounding incorporation of the Bill of Rights through the due process clause has, historically, been most closely linked to issues surrounding the rights of the criminally accused.[62] The Warren Court made dramatic doctrinal innovations in a long list of cases involving right to counsel, search and seizure, coerced

---

61. This position is associated with the work of Catherine MacKinnon and Andrea Dworkin. Canada has adopted an approach that reflects their influence but in actual practice, it has resulted in some feminist writings being censored. See Jeffrey Toobin, "Annals of Law: X-Rated," *The New Yorker* 3 October 1994.

62. See *Hurtado v. California*, 110 U.S. 516 (1884); *Maxwell v. Dow* 176 U.S. 581 (1900); *Twining v. New Jersey*, 211 U.S. 78 (1908); *Palko v. Connecticut*, 302 U.S. 319 (1937); *Adamson v. California*, 332 U.S. 46 (1947); *Rochin v. California*, 342 U.S. 165 (1952).

confessions, self-incrimination, trial by jury, and police interrogation of suspects.[63]

This area has already seen extensive doctrinal alterations from the Burger and Rehnquist Courts that softens--some would say subverts--many important Warren Court innovations. Looking at this body of doctrine today, one finds that on the one hand, the *Gideon*[64] holding still is followed and attorneys are now routinely provided for indigent defendants accused of crimes. *Miranda*[65] warnings are still (usually) required and persons arrested are routinely told (even in movies and on television) that they have the right to remain silent, that they have the right to have an attorney present, and that if they are indigent, an attorney will be provided for them. And the states must still (on the whole) adhere to the reasonable search and seizure rule under threat of otherwise having the fruits of the search excluded from evidence at trial. On the other hand, it is no secret that the exceptions to the rules are now many and significant.[66] Although the major holdings of the Warren Court, such as the *Miranda v. Arizona*[67] rules and the search and seizure exclusionary rule,[68] are technically still intact, they have been much altered. Today it is essentially the case that a confession acquired without giving *Miranda* warnings may still be admissible unless it was actually coerced. Similarly, evidence gathered in violation of the Fourth Amendment's search and seizure provisions may be admitted if the violation of constitutional requirements resulted from a good faith error.

---

63. See among others, *Gideon v. Wainwright*, 372 U.S. 335 (1963); *Mapp v. Ohio*, 367 U.S. 643 (1961); *Katz v. United States*, 389 U.S. 347 (1967); *Malloy v. Hogan*, 378 U.S. 1 (1964); *Escobedo v. Illinois* (1964); *Miranda v. Arizona*, 384 U.S. 436 (1966); *Duncan v. Louisiana*, 391 U.S. 145 (1968).

64. 372 U.S. 335 (1963).

65. 384 U.S. 436 (1966).

66. See for example, *U.S. v. Leon*, 468 U.S. 897 (1984) establishing a "good faith" exception to the search and seizure exclusionary rule, and *Oregon v. Olmstead*, 470 U.S. 298 (1985) holding that an admission made prior to the giving of *Miranda* warnings does not invalidate a later warned admission. See also the public safety exception to *Miranda* in *New York v. Quarles*, 467 U.S. 649 (1984). Still, even today the Court continues to set limits on the police that would have been unthinkable before the Warren Court era. Thus the Court recently held that the State of Wisconsin can make no blanket exception to the knock-and-announce requirement for felony drug investigations. *Richards v. Wisconsin*, 117 S.Ct. 1416 (1997).

67. 384 U.S. 436 (1966).

68. See *Mapp v. Ohio*, 367 U.S. 643 (1961).

But the criminal justice system has changed fundamentally too. Nationwide, many elements of the system are much more professional than they were thirty years ago, and it is not clear they will cease following many due process standards that are hallmarks of that professionalism regardless of the fact that current judicial doctrine no longer always requires it explicitly. This is true despite the continuing controversy that surrounds constitutional doctrines in the area of criminal procedure originally formulated by the Warren Court and the controversy that surrounds the issue of crime in general.

The major continuing doctrinal difference in the approach of post-Warren Courts has involved the claim of deference to federalism. The Burger Court resisted the Warren Court's tendency to find constitutional violation in shocking or unfair abuses not clearly tied to established doctrine or process. The Rehnquist Court continued and developed this stance. The result is that there are no federal constitutional remedies for many instances of shocking official behavior, and thus those offended are limited to the variable remedies available in some states but not others. This difference, lacking the doctrinal sweep of many Warren Court thrusts and often hidden in technicalities, highlights the fundamental conflict between the Warren Court and its successors. It carries reverberations of an underlying conflict in perspectives, discussed later in this book, that have warred throughout the twentieth century.

The Warren Court's doctrinal innovation with the most ultimately controversial impact was *Griswold v. Connecticut*[69] in which the Court first announced the right to privacy. The Court was criticized by many scholars at the time for finding a right nowhere explicitly mentioned in the text of the Constitution and then putting forth several different theories for its constitutional source. However, it was not until the Burger Court expanded privacy to a right to abortion that the criticism became truly intense.

In terms of significant doctrinal innovation, easily the most activist Supreme Court decision since *Brown v. Board of Education*[70] was *Roe v. Wade*[71]--the abortion case. It was a Burger Court decision and Chief Justice Burger himself joined in it, though he changed his mind about *Roe* by the end of his term. The decision in *Roe v. Wade* was written by Burger's old friend and law school classmate, the "Minnesota twin" and former counsel to the Mayo Clinic, Harry Blackmun.

---

69. 381 U.S. 479 (1965).
70. 347 U.S. 483 (1954).
71. 410 U.S. 113 (1973).

Indeed, a large part of the concern over the legitimacy of modern judicial activism often seems to come down to *Roe v. Wade*.[72] It is no exaggeration to say that the preponderance of the recent and extensive debate and commentary over judicial activism has really been motivated by discontent over that decision. There are many reasons for this. First of all, the decision flies in the face of the religious beliefs of many Americans. It is a fact that the Constitution does not mention privacy, let alone abortion. Until shortly before the decision came down, virtually no one of prominence had ever seriously argued that abortion was a constitutional right. Furthermore, there was little previous doctrinal groundwork laid before the sweeping decision came down. The political process seemed to grapple effectively with the issue without judicial intervention; several states (most notably New York) were acting to liberalize their abortion laws on their own in the early 1970s. Finally, the last straw for many critics is that the decision is so detailed that in their eyes it is too much like a piece of legislation.

Certainly this dramatic piece of Burger Court activism was not really anticipated. When President Nixon attempted to move the Court to the right in the late 1960s and early 1970s, some moderation of, or even reversal of, Warren Court doctrinal development was reasonably predicted. The abortion decision, whatever else it was, was the kind of audacious expansion of rights that one scarcely expected from a Court that was self-consciously trying to move to the right.

Many do not realize that *Roe* is not a Warren Court decision. *Griswold* is, but as Judge Robert Bork discovered in his confirmation hearings over his ultimately unsuccessful nomination for the Supreme Court, while the American people and their representatives are divided about abortion, most hold rather solidly positive views about privacy. Here the Warren Court's legacy seems secure whatever happens to *Roe*.

Even if *Roe* is ultimately overruled or the scope of the constitutional right to abortion is significantly restricted, the result will not be the disappearance of abortion from America. That is because, again, American society has changed in many fundamental ways. Today, a large part of the country sees abortion as not only a privacy issue but a gender equality issue.[73] If the Court ever returns abortion to the states, something that at this writing seems

72. 410 U.S. 113 (1973).

73. Justice Ginsburg is correct in her expressed view that the abortion decision could have been grounded in equal protection as well as privacy.

increasingly unlikely, many states will maintain liberal abortion policies.

Indeed while the abortion decision is grounded in the right to privacy, it is, in fact, fundamentally a women's rights decision. It was the American society of the early 1970s that felt the first stunning impact of the contemporary women's movement. It was not until this early 1970s period that the U.S. Supreme Court ever struck down laws that classified on the basis of gender. Whatever the other rights the Warren Court may have developed or expanded, it did nothing at all for the rights of women. It was the Burger Court that first extended some constitutional protection to gender discrimination, something that the Rehnquist Court has continued in a limited manner.[74] The gradual and somewhat unpredictable development of the "semi-suspect" classification is less than most women's rights advocates would like. Nevertheless it is these more conservative Courts that innovated in this vital area.

In *Reed v. Reed*,[75] the Court struck down a law giving absolute preference to men as administrators of estates by viewing gender as an "ordinary," but in this instance, unreasonable classification under the Court's then prevalent two-tier approach. This approach viewed legislative classifications as either ordinary and presumed valid, or suspect and presumed invalid. Since the result in *Reed* really could not be plausibly sustained under classic "ordinary" analysis, the next case, *Frontiero v. Richardson*[76] found four justices willing to treat gender as "suspect." However, this situation, one vote short of a majority, was the historic "high point" matched by no subsequent case. Instead, over the years gender has come to be seen as an intermediate or "semi-suspect" classification subject to greater scrutiny than ordinary classifications, but something less than the strict scrutiny of "suspect" classifications.

What were arguably the two most important areas of post-Warren Court activism, abortion rights and gender classification, involved important doctrinal innovations that were related to an underlying change in American society as dramatic and far-reaching as any we have experienced. The rapid rise of feminism and women's rights concerns to a serious position on the mainstream American agenda, the entry of most women into the workforce and the routine pursuit of serious professional careers by the preponderance of upper middle-class

---

74 Most notably in *U.S. v. Virginia*, 116 S.Ct. 2264 (1996).

75. 404 U.S. 71 (1971).

76. 411 U.S. 677 (1973).

women have all been remarkable developments.[77] Evidently, even conservative justices evidently could not be unaffected by so profound a social change.

Because the doctrinal innovations by conservative Courts in the area of women's rights were much less than most liberals would have wished, the activism has gone largely uncriticized except from some feminists who deem it inadequate. But clearly the recognition of constitutional protection for women was activism. The equal protection clause had existed for more than a century without offering any protection whatsoever against discriminatory gender classifications; all prior challenges had been rejected.[78] The limited process of recognition that began in the early 1970s was a sudden, innovative, creative (if somewhat confused) development of doctrine in ways that contradicted all previous understandings. It involved a vigorous assertion of judicial authority in contravention of established legislative pronouncement.

The societal change that accompanied the rather sudden recognition of constitutional protection against some forms of gender discrimination was quite striking and doubtless influenced the Court. If the Supreme Court does not always follow the election returns, it is certainly a part of the larger society and cannot easily remain unaffected by fundamental social and cultural change.

More important, activism and doctrinal innovation that reflects such fundamental change is the kind most likely to survive over the long run. With the continued rise of women within the institutional structures of American society, including, of course, the Supreme Court itself, these particular kinds of doctrinal innovations from the Burger and Rehnquist Courts are likely not only to survive but further to develop significantly. Indeed, if these societal trends continue and the political, social, and economic influence of women continues to increase, it is hard to imagine the Court continuing to hold out against making gender a suspect classification.

Despite all the notable efforts of the Burger and Rehnquist Courts aimed at altering the Warren Court's legacy, as of this writing the preponderance of the Warren Court's major doctrinal innovations still remain intact. This is so despite a sustained attack upon the Warren Court by four Republican presidents--Richard Nixon, Gerald Ford, Ronald Reagan, and George Bush--over a period approximating

---

77. For a summary of relevant social developments see chapter 9 of Rosenberg, *The Hollow Hope*.

78. *Bradwell v. Illinois* (16 Wall.) 130 (1873); *Minor v. Happersett*, (21 Wall.) 162 (1875); *Goesart v. Cleary* 335 U.S. 464 (1948).

four years. (President Jimmy Carter had no opportunity to appoint Supreme Court justices during his four year Democratic interregnum.)

While the election of Democrat Bill Clinton as president in 1992, and his subsequent appointments of Ruth Bader Ginsberg and Stephen Breyer, has had some moderating influence, the Court remains sharply divided on many issues. Indeed, several recent close decisions of the Court that featured a conservative majority adjusting doctrine were attacked by liberals as shocking conservative activism. The controversy over judicial activism in general and the legacy of the unique activism of the Warren Court era in particular, continues unabated. Much of the scholarly effort in recent times has focused upon the question of the legitimacy of judicial activism.

three/ The Question of the Legitimacy of Judicial Activism

It is no secret that the last two decades have seen an extensive scholarly attack on judical activism. Most recent writing about the subject has focused on normative analysis of the exercise of judicial power in a democracy. Yet such attacks are incapable of resolving the normative dilemma upon which the effort is premised and, as a result, it has clearly reached a point of diminishing intellectual returns.

There is an intellectual context both to periods of activism and to the subsequent reaction to them. It can be found in the constant intellectual interaction between the pronouncements of justices and the comments of others. Traditionally scholarship of all kinds, and law school commentary in particular, has contributed to the intellectual context. Increasingly print journalism and the broadcast media also have a major impact.

It is probably significant that both principal eras of activism in this century were accompanied by sharp ideological polarizations within the nation and on the Court. It may be recalled too that the high point of Warren Court activism in the mid-1960s was also the high point of the effort of quantitative political science, epitomized in the work of Glendon Schubert, to demonstrate that the decisions of the Court were predictable, which they were, though as many pointed out at the time, one did not really need sophisticated quantitative techniques to know this. The decisions were so predictable because there was, somewhat uniquely in that 1960s period, a clarity to the ideological divisions and doctrinal conflicts that is much less available today. The time in the mid-1960s when liberalism was in the saddle in all three branches was not a long period, but it was in many ways a unique one.

While the conflicts of the century's first era of activism contained some elements of predictability at certain points in time, that cannot be said of other elements of these drawn out and varied conflicts. As to the states in particular, the Court was then asserting the right to review the reasonableness of economic regulation, which implied that some regulations would be found wanting and some satisfactory, and from the standpoint of critics, the Court's unpredictability was a major part of the problem.

It does seem likely that a supportive, dominant ideological climate in the society that is reflected on the Court probably gives the Court a kind of self-confidence (critics might say arrogance) to undertake an activist program.[1] Certainly, by the end of the nineteenth century there were powerful and dominant ideological currents in place. Industrial capitalism had transformed societies here and in Europe. The European powers had established important empires in the non-White world, and America too had formally acquired colonial possessions. Social Darwinism was a powerful intellectual current, and theories of White racial superiority were respectable in major universities in Europe and America. Perhaps these helped shape the Court that formed in the late 1800s when Jim Crow was being implemented across the South and the Supreme Court was ratifying it. But any direct cause and effect relationship is hard to establish. Of course, no less an authority than Justice Oliver Wendell Holmes alluded to the majority's finding Herbert Spencer's *Social Statics* in the Fourteenth Amendment in his famous *Lochner* dissent.[2] Perhaps both university dogma and Supreme Court doctrine were reflections of broader international social and political developments of the period.

---

1. It is helpful in providing that self-confidence, but obviously a dominant ideological climate reflected on the Court does not guarantee activism or we might have more of it currently. On the other hand, one might also argue that the current situation still lacks a really dominant ideological climate. Our politics today are more ideological and there is a diversity of competing and shifting ideological alignments, but no real dominance--yet.

Ideological climates in the sense meant here are primarily matters of elite or "establishment" belief; they are not necessarily reflected in Gallop polls. Even as to the elite or "establishment,,"the claim would be of a general attitude, and not that each and every Supreme Court decision will be demanded or explicitly supported.

2. *Lochner v. New York* 146 U.S. 46, 74 (1904)

Throughout this period there were important countercurrents, but it took several decades for a new intellectual order to achieve dominance in America. By midcentury, this had occurred and one plausibly could argue that the intellectual context of the late 1940s and early 1950s helped shape Warren Court activism. The doctrines that dominated the American social sciences by the 1940s were very different from those that dominated in the prior era.[3] By the same token it is less than clear whether the dominance of this nonracist anthropology and social science in America's elite universities by the time of *Brown* [4] is a cause of *Brown*, or whether both are the result of fundamental political and social changes that came to America two decades earlier, reinforced by the lessons of the Second World War.

There are other specific changes that had occurred before *Brown* that also seem relevant. There was a greater diversity among the elite professoriat in major universities as different kinds of Americans, and European refugees, began to enter in large numbers. The GI Bill produced mass higher education in America for the first time, exposing large numbers of individuals who were to become members of America's enlarged post-war upper middle class to the more racially enlightened ideas of this mid-century university professoriat. Radio and then television enabled Americans to know each other, to hear, and then see each other on a regular basis.

On the other hand, some important law school commentary was not really supportive of *Brown* or seemed to find some aspects of the decision awkward.[5] On other issues too, the impact of the academy was problematic. What is one to make of the impact of McCarthyism on the academy and then on the Court? Did the reaction to it really produce any major breakthrough in free speech doctrine? Did the academy do much to impact church and state doctrine, reapportionment doctrine, privacy or criminal procedure? The evidence is thin on most of these; and on reapportionment, much of the immediate academic reaction was negative.

Certainly the relationship between ideas and government policies and actions is not all a one-way street. Of course, ideas do matter and

---

3. See Ashley Montagu, *The Concept of Race* (Glencoe, Ill.: Free Press of Glencoe, 1964).

4. *Brown v. Board of Education*, 347 U.S. 483 (1954)

5. See Herbert Wechsler, "Toward Neutral Principals of Constitutional Law," *Harvard Law Review* 73 (1959), 1; Alexander Bickel, "The Original Understanding and the Segregation Decision," *Harvard Law Review* 69 (1955), 1.

they do have an impact on society and government, including the Supreme Court. But the belief that ideas always come first and simply through their "power" change politics and society, or produce new Court doctrine, may be seen as primarily a conceit of the idea-producing class. It is more complicated than that. It is apparent that certain ideas, particularly political, social and economic ideas, do not come to prominence and dominance just because they are "proven true." In many instances it is because they give voice to or reflect the aspirations of, or explain or rationalize something of significance that has actually occurred to those with new influence in the politics and the society of a given period. In that sense many ideas, and the Court doctrine sometimes associated with them, may be seen, or come to be seen, as ideological and time-bound. These ideas are more a product of their times than a cause of them. Yet even where this is so, there may still be elements of the ideas that have a deeper validity and longer-term significance.

In recent decades, the scholarly reaction to the Warren Court's activism has been almost exclusively normative. The effort has been to show that the Court's activism itself was wrong or right--that the Court did or did not abuse its power by using it to excess. Some would see this effort as ideological. The thrust of much of it has been primarily conservative, a reaction to the liberal activism of the 1960s and early 1970s. Some of it came to pass as a result of changes in American politics: the decay of the political coalition that provided a climate of support for the broad thrust (if not all the details) of Warren Court activism, and the gradual coming to power of a new conservative coalition.

These observers of the Supreme Court and the lower federal courts during the past three decades have shared a sense that there is something intellectually unsatisfying about the great expansion of rights and liberties that have been among the principal objects of these courts' attention during this period. Of course, all who have been moved to comment do not share the same motive: some seek to provide legitimacy for the judicial activism of the post-war decades and some seek to undercut it. Nearly all find some awkwardness in the nondemocratic aspects of the practice, yet all recognize it as venerable in the American system.

Most recent commentators on judicial review and the limits of judicial activism seek the "correct" way to appropriately cabin the "plain words" of the Constitution, most of which are so broad and so sweeping as to render almost nothing clearly precluded. (After all, "Freedom of Speech," "Freedom of Religion," "Due Process of Law," and

"Equal Protection of the Laws" are phrases that offer precious little specific and practical guidance to judges or commentators.)

Those who are unhappy with the libertarian and egalitarian values reflected in the decisions normally manifest their dissatisfaction with an attack on the courts as excessively active and by a demand for judicial restraint within what they deem proper limits. Even those who are sympathetic and who believe that the kinds of conflicts the courts are resolving are their proper business often claim to find something inadequate in the intellectual framework for these activities and suggest an appropriate substitute framework.

Despite these differences of solution, one could say that there is usually a common intellectual approach to resolving the normative problem of controlling the process of interpreting the words of the Constitution--what might be termed a prototypical pattern. First the commentator creates an abstraction in reference to the words of the Constitution. Next he or she refers to the abstraction for guidance and control over the use of the words and then "argues" with himself or herself over the details of the abstraction. (This serves to create in the reader a sense of the abstraction as an effective means of control while simultaneously getting the reader to take for granted what might otherwise be the real point in issue: the sufficiency and appropriateness of the particular abstraction as a control device.)

Thus rights-oriented theory takes rights seriously by abstracting and reshaping a right in philosophical terms that require, or at least rationalize, a particular agenda. Structuralists abstract structure from the Constitution as a whole and argue that this structure dictates appropriate results. Original intentionalists would argue that they trade in history, not abstraction. They "discover" an "actual" historical intent as a context within which the words may have meaning. But whether original intent is really objectively discoverable in any meaningful sense is highly debatable. What is found is undoubtedly a historical abstraction with a bit of actual history mixed in here and there that "permits" some results and "forbids" others.

There is little that is really new in the fights that have been fought in the past two decades. Most of the arguments and positions had been developed in earlier versions as part of earlier confrontations. Still, the changing political climate, new and divisive constitutional activism (most notably surrounding the abortion issue), and the rise to prominence of a new generation of constitutional scholars has brought renewed vigor to the controversy.

Most prominent, or perhaps most prolific, of the original intentionalists of the last two decades has been Raoul Berger who produced several books as entries on the side of fundamentalist, "original intentionalist" interpretation. Berger's work came to symbolize an approach that has gained increasing adherence in conservative quarters. This has been true even though there have been prior times in this century where original intentionalism has been used for liberal ends and activism has accomplished conservative objectives.[6]

Berger's work is represented best by his book, *Government by Judiciary.* Here Berger criticizes the Supreme Court's "continuing revision of the Constitution under the guise of interpretation." He feels that those who defend such practices and see them as judicial statesmanship do so because their "predilections are mirrored" in the Court's decisions. He holds that "courts no less than presidents" must adhere to limits in a democratic system. He then proceeds to undertake his own historical study of the framing of the Fourteenth Amendment in an effort to determine concretely the intentions of its framers, for Berger holds that for the Court to go beyond these explicit and knowable intentions in interpreting the clauses of the amendment is to go beyond the Court's legitimate role in our system.

Berger believes that the records of the Thirty-ninth Congress that framed the amendment are free from often leveled criticism of historical records as enigmatic, sparse or cryptic. He instead uses words like "unequivocal" and "incontrovertible," yet fails to grapple with many of the subtleties of his claims. In some sense, of course, that is because his approach has an insistent simplicity that rejects complications that others see as subtle, as nothing but evasion of clear-cut truth. Although Berger works hard to create an overall systematic theory of the meaning and intention that underlies the amendment, his kind of "common sense,""they meant what the said" approach has many difficulties.[7]

Congressman John Bingham was the leading mover in formulating the Fourteenth Amendment, and we have some sense of what motivated him. Yet there are contradictions and ambiguities in his statements in the record of the proceedings of the Joint Committee and in what Congress did when it received the drafts of the amendment from the

---

6. The most notable efforts to use original intentionalism for liberal objectives were the voluminous historical efforts that accompanied the recusitation of reconstruction civil rights statutes by New Deal and post-New Deal Courts.

7. Raoul Berger, *Government by Judiciary: The Transformation of the Fourteenth Amendment* (Cambridge, Mass.: Harvard University Press, 1977), 1,2,7.

committee. Indeed, it can be said that no really coherent theory of what the Amendment was supposed to do can be extracted from the record for a variety of reasons, not the least of which is that the mentality that was brought to bear then had some different focuses and premises from ours today.

Berger's affirmative efforts at explaining what the amendment was allegedly intended to accomplish is rather perfunctory, lacking in depth of analysis and far less persuasive than his presentation of evidence that he sees as undermining specific instances of judicial activism. His use of evidence is often selective and many of his interpretive judgments, such as his insistence that the record clearly supports a narrow conception of the privileges and immunities clause, are highly debatable, even arbitrary. But some of his other points are valid within limits .

Thus it is probably true that section one of the amendment was not originally intended to deal with suffrage. It does seem that the committee was struggling ambivalently with its desire to enfranchise the Negro; they were surely interested in the votes enfranchisement would bring the Republicans in the South, yet concerned by the opposition this might bring elsewhere in the country. The framers also did not intend to prohibit segregated schools or miscegenation, and it is also true, as Berger argues, that committed exponents of broad abolitionist constitutional theories did not command an amending majority, though it hardly follows that their views and influence can therefore be promptly put aside. But the problem with original intent conceived of in the way Berger approaches it is that although the record of the Joint Committee may seem clear on a specific question, such as not supporting suffrage, it is most definitely not clear on many other issues connected with the amendment.

If you approach the Fourteenth Amendment by isolating certain issues and asking narrowly for evidence about intent, you may in some instances succeed in finding it and in demonstrating that something the modern Supreme Court has done goes beyond contemporary expressions of intent at the time of passage. But it is also true that if you ask about other issues you will not succeed, and if you undertake a systematic inquiry you will conclude that a truly coherent systematic intent is available only to a very limited degree. The reason for this is not, as fundamentalists would have it, because precious little was intended, but because of significant contradictions in the evidence and critical disagreements among the amending factions that cannot be compromised or reconciled, but which nevertheless failed to stop them from voting for the amendment at the time.[8]

Close examination of the historical record produces a realization of the limits to the coherence of the conception that the framers brought to their work and gives rise to deep skepticism about the legitimacy of adhering to intent in isolated cases, which cannot be systematically reconciled within the larger problem of the meaning of the amendment as a whole. Some might reasonably feel that it relieves us of the obligation to follow isolated pieces of expressed intention, which may or may not be consistent with each other assuming, for the sake of argument, that we have such an obligation in the first place. Original intentionalists are likely to downplay the importance of this concern, but other people are likely to give it great weight.

Other more telling objections have been rendered to the original intent approach. The first is that even if the intent of the framers was totally knowable and remains usable today, how do we know they wanted us to follow it? There is a possible conundrum here: what if their intent was that we not follow original intent? To put the matter more usefully, there is little reason to suppose that the framers expected to bind us to their precise conception of the scope of what they were doing. They doubtless expected us to adhere to their purposes and to respect the principles and concepts they were expressing, but to say this is to leave a great deal of discretion indeed.

Another criticism of the strict original intent approach asks: if we are to be bound by a laundry list of specific "do's and don'ts" in regard to a phrase like "equal protection of the laws;" why did its framers not put that laundry list into the amendment? In other sections of the Fourteenth Amendment, after all, they were quite precise, and the provisions in many state constitutions are extremely detailed. There is in fact no rule that requires that provisions of constitutional amendments must use vague, general terms.

---

8. See Alexander Bickel,"The Original Understanding"; Archibald Cox, "Foreword: Constitutional Adjudication and the Promotion of Human Rights," *Harvard Law Review* 80 (1966), 1; L. B. Frantz, "Congressional Power to Enforce the Fourteenth Amendment Against Private Acts," *Yale Law Journal* 73 (1964), 1353; Howard J. Graham, "Our 'Declaratory' Fourteenth Amendment," *Stanford Law Review* 7 (1954), 3; Robert Harris, *The Search for Equality* (Baton Rouge: Louisiana State University Press, 1960); Joseph James, *The Framing of the Fourteenth Amendment* (Urbana,Ill.: University of Illinois Press, 1956); Jacobus TenBroek, *Equal Under Law* (New York: Collier Books, 1965).

By the 1860s, the idea that the Supreme Court might well be taking general phrases of the Constitution and interpreting them aggressively was well understood. Indeed, many framers had roots in anti-slavery politics and felt that the Court had handled the issues that had concerned them most very badly. If the framers did not want the Court to ever carry the amendment beyond their specific original intent (i.e., no suffrage matters, no school integration, etc.), why didn't they say so? There were questions about these matters at the time and they must have realized that a hundred years into the future, it could be possible that the Court or Congress would take a general phrase like "equal protection of the laws" and develop it beyond their then present intention.

Being politicians, they were doubtless more concerned with papering over issues than in highlighting them. The advantage to vague phrases is that the various factions necessary to obtain a constitutional amending majority both in Congress and the states can get behind them and read into them whatever empowerments and entitlements they seek. The proponents, with perhaps different ideas of where "equal protection of the laws" might end up 150 years in the future--assuming that they had the imagination, time, and inclination to ponder that question at all--would have found it sufficient to say, truthfully, that given then current meanings and political contexts, the amendment would do this and not do that--for now.

Where original intentionalist analysis breaks down is that while reading the record does sustain, for example, the claim that the leading figures in the move to enact the Fourteenth Amendment probably would have said "no, this amendment will not accomplish public school integration," they would have only meant presently or in the then immediate future. If someone farsighted were to have asked, "given the language of this Amendment, could these things come to pass through interpretation in the distant future, and is it your intention to absolutely preclude these possibilities and to have the future bound by such present specific intentions," they would have replied something like, "yes, these things could perhaps happen in the far distant future, and no, we would not wish to absolutely preclude them, or we would do so explicitly, but we would rather not talk about this now, thank you."

Indeed, while the imposition of intentionalist views upon the original founding fathers has a case to be made for it--not a conclusive case but at least a case--the imposition of such views upon the framers of the Fourteenth Amendment actually borders on the farfetched. These people, even the relatively "conservative" among them, were not true fundamentalists who would hold voters, legislators, presidents, and

Supreme Courts to the precise details of the mentalities encompassed in covenants entered into by extraordinary amending majorities in times past, as might be revealed in subsequent objective examinations of the historical record. Quite the opposite, many of the radical Republican leaders were men with very strong personal senses of right and wrong and a very quick disposition to read their moral sensibilities into the old Constitution, regardless of the historical record, and they constituted a significant portion of the amending majority.

Although Berger and the other original intentionalists have responded to criticism of their work, it is notable that it is almost exclusively on their own terms. It is dismissive of the arguments of critics who read the historical record differently but do not really confront the broader criticism of the approach. Original intentionalists tend to be so affronted by what they see as the unrestricted exercise of judicial power and so confident in the corrective qualities of their approach and interpretation that they seem unable to appreciate what others see as its serious limitations.

An additional problem for the most strict intentionalists lies in the fact that other prominent original intentionalists, such as Robert Bork, are more willing than Berger to accept the proposition that intention can sometimes be abstracted or conceived of at a higher level of generality involving purposes or principles that may support an interpretation that is contrary to the probable or expressed intention of framers in congressional debates. As critics have often pointed out, this slightly greater flexibility serves both to highlight the rigidity of someone like Berger while simultaneously suggesting that original intentionalism's proponents can be somewhat arbitrary in its application.

The "common sense, plain-talking American" aspects of original intentionalism are, of course, undermined by differences of this kind. One can plausibly say that the framers of the equal protection clause intended what they say they intended on the historical record, assuming that can be established, and nothing more. One can say with equal plausibility that they intended to make Blacks equal in the receipt of essential government-conferred rights and services, and that our conception of what is essential has properly evolved over one hundred years to include some additional things. Alternately one can plausibly say that the framers simply spoke in the amendment of persons not being denied equal protection of the laws that placed the idea of equality into the Constitution in a very general way. Perhaps their conception of the persons and the protection that mattered was much more limited than ours is, but if the standard is expressed at a high level of generality, as it clearly was, the fact that our conception of what fulfills it is (we believe) much more developed than theirs does not invalidate it as contrary to original intention.

Thus, although a fundamental rights advocate like Ronald Dworkin is often placed at the opposite pole from the original intentionalists, he would argue that his approach is properly faithful to the intentions and purposes of the framers of the Constitution and the amendments. He sees these as encompassing fundamental rights values that can be abstracted to a high level and then applied successfully to concrete modern problems.

In Dworkin's view "it is wrong to attack the Warren Court . . . on the ground that it failed to treat the Constitution as a binding text. On the contrary, if we wish to treat fidelity to the text as an overriding requirement of constitutional interpretation, then it is the conservative critics of the Warren Court who are at fault, because their philosophy ignores the direction to face issues of moral principle that the logic of the text demands."[9]

Such commentary is criticized by many as essentially ideologically liberal, appealing to those who are trying to rationalize their agenda by "finding" its values in the Constitution. The approach can be characterized as manipulative because the level of abstraction selected for application to the analysis of any particular issue is a somewhat arbitrary process, and the level selected rather clearly tends to determine the outcome of the analysis.

Because the philosophical methods most rights-based proponents use are often very complex, neither they nor their deficiencies are easily reducible to brief examples. Still, consider that if through a process of abstraction, we establish that the equal protection clause is basically about assisting members of the formerly enslaved and still

---

9. Ronald Dworkin, *Taking Rights Seriously* (Cambridge, Mass: Harvard University Press, 1977), 136.

Michael Perry holds the view that the Constitution, like a sacred religious document, is interpreted properly by reference to the values of the interpretive community that has developed around it over two centuries. If the Court interprets actively and at a high level of abstraction within this interpretive tradition, Perry believes its actions to be valid. See for example, Michael J. Perry, *The Constitution, The Courts and Human Rights* (New Haven: Yale University Press, 1982).

Sanford Levinson considers the Constitution as part of America's civil religion with a "Protestant" and "Catholic" tradition. See his *Constitutional Faith* (Princeton, N.J.: Princeton University Press, 1988), 41 where Levinson holds that the search for consensus about the Constitution is "chimerical."

disadvantaged Black race to achieve meaningful equality, we may therefore find the clause fully compatible with quota-oriented affirmative action programs. But if our process of abstraction establishes that the clause is basically about extending to all individual persons the same right of access to services and opportunities without regard to race, creed, color, or national origin, we may find the clause incompatible with many current affirmative action programs.

In fact, plausible and elaborate processes of reasoning can be set forth at either of these levels of abstraction (or at any of several others) and, as mentioned above, the level selected is really both somewhat arbitrary and simultaneously determinative of one's ultimate intellectual destination and conclusions. Indeed, where conservatives adopt the fundamental rights approach, they are likely to find themselves the object of criticism by its liberal proponents.[10]

Though the approaches already discussed have had considerable impact upon the debate, arguably the most influential book of recent years on constitutional interpretation is *Democracy and Distrust* by John Hart Ely. Ely rejects both what he terms "clause bound interpretivism" and the "fundamental values" approach of the rights theorists. He turns instead to the famous preferred position footnote of *U.S. v. Carolene Products.*[11]

Stressing process over substantive values, Ely argues that policing the process of representation--striking down practices that interfere with democratic processes or that are examples of majorities denying participatory rights to groups and individuals--is the legitimate function of the Court. These conditions exist "when (1) the ins are choking off the channels of political change to ensure that they will stay in and the outs stay out, or (2) though no one is actually denied a voice or a vote, representatives beholden to an effective majority are systematically disadvantaging some minority out of simple hostility or a prejudiced refusal to recognize commonalities of interest, and thereby denying that minority the protection afforded other groups by a representative system."[12] Ely sees clearing the channels of political change as an allied obligation; he sees protecting speech and related political rights as facilitating the representation of minorities.

---

10. See Ronald Dworkin reviewing Charles Fried, *Order and Law: Arguing the Reagan Revolution--A Firsthand Account* (New York: Simon and Schuster, 1991) in *The New York Review of Books 28,* no. 13 (July 18, 1991): 23.

11. 304 U.S. 144,152-53 n. 4 (1938).

12. John Hart Ely, *Democracy and Distrust* (Cambridge, Mass.: Harvard University Press, 1980). 103.

There is much to be said for Ely's theory as a rationale for most of what the Supreme Court was up to during the Warren Court years and the period immediately thereafter. But Ely's broader claim that he is offering a definitive theory for controlling all judicial review and defining the contours of legitimacy is less convincing.

It does not seem, for example, that his approach and its emphasis would provide justices with much real guidance in deciding free speech questions rather far removed from the political as it is usually understood. Is it an abuse of the political process to impose majority aesthetic tastes on the minority that wants to express itself? In issues that actually arise in aesthetic speech, are not considerations of reasonably coherent cultural group identity and/or its symbolic self-expression often involved, along with, at least ultimate, political ramifications?[13] Is not the passage of any law that impinges on some group's speech, even when the speech in question is far removed from what we normally consider political, in some sense acting to block the channels of political change? Since these kinds of indirect considerations can arguably be asserted in virtually every situation depending on how one looks at it, the Ely approach seems inadequate as a controlling theory for judicial review.

By the same token, Ely suggests that the abortion decision is outside the scope of legitimacy under his approach. Yet since the decision clearly empowers a group--women (while not technically a minority, they have rather clearly been subject historically to disadvantages through the political process that has impaired their effective representation and participation in our society), it might be seen as within his theory. The empowerment is indirect but on a matter quite fundamental to the course of a woman's entire life, and thus as a practical matter, her ability to undertake major political activity.

Ely believes that while elements of women's historical situation justify treating them as covered by the preferred position doctrine, their majority status and lack of insularity makes him reluctant to carry such protection too far. Indeed, his "second look" approach, if applied to abortion, would support reversal of *Roe* and a return of the issue to the state legislatures.

One can come to this conclusion, of course, but one can just as easily argue that the nature of nature and the human condition requires us to look at the situation of women as somewhat different from other

---

13. The postmodernist, poststructuralist approach to literary and aesthetic criticism finds the political in all such expression. For a general overview of the debate over the effects of such views on university campuses, see Paul Berman, ed.,*Debating PC*. (New York: Dell, 1992).

"minorities." Or one could argue that the relevant "minority" is not all women, but rather that large number of women, but still a numerical minority, who want to seriously undertake political and societal activity on the same terms as the politically dominant White male group. One can plausibly argue that in a very real and meaningful sense, such full participation is denied these women without the ability to decide the life-dominating reproductive issue.[14] In truth, whether Ely's approach really decides any hard questions depends on how one approaches his approach.

Ely's discussion of how the right to travel fits into his theory and his notion that his theory is a kind of antitrust approach is coherent; it describes quite accurately much of what the Warren Court's doctrine did within the context of changing pluralism in America. Ely's theory is most valuable as a convincing description of the specific intellectual framework within which the most important business of the Court has taken place in recent decades.

It is both unnecessary and incorrect to take this theory and extend it to the point of requiring that Court activity that is not clearly encompassed by the theory is thereby invalid. Providing previously disenfranchised or otherwise disadvantaged groups with meaningfull equality is indeed what the Court has been primarily doing, and its activity has been valid and coherent. But that is not all that the Court has been doing and if it did or does something else on occasion, this something else is therefore not automatically invalid.

Although there are numerous variations and subcategories, these then, are the three principal normative approaches that have commanded attention in recent years. The limits to all these efforts to delineate the proper scope of judicial review are best expressed in "The Fundamental Rights Controversy: Essential Contradictions of Normative Constitutional Scholarship" by Paul Brest.[15] Though written in 1981, nothing has undermined the basic insight, not to mention the sophisticated common sense of its conclusions.

Brest holds that "the controversy over the legitimacy of judicial review in a democratic polity . . . is essentially incoherent and unresolvable." He argues that the approach of each commentator can be

14. For an argument that Ely's approach could be used to support *Roe* see Archibald Cox, Book Review, *Harvard Law Review* 94 (1981), 700, 709-711. Ely is criticized for "theoretical incoherence" by David A.J. Richards. See his "Liberalism, Free Speech and Justice for Minorities" in *In Harm's Way*, J. Coleman and A. Buchanan, eds. (New York: Cambridge University Press, 1994).

15. *Yale Law Journal* 90 (1981), 1063.

used to contradict his approach. Thus as to Berger's original intention, it remains extremely doubtful that the framers of the Fourteenth Amendment intended such strict faithfulness to their specific intentions.

Ely's process-oriented strategy outlined in *Democracy and Distrust* and designed to avoid the problem of values cannot avoid value choices. The rights theorists disagree on specifics and this stems at least in part from the arbitrariness of the level of abstraction selected in approaching any specific issue. In the end, Brest feels that rights-oriented approaches are haunted by the "ghost" of *Lochner*[16] and properly so.

According to Brest, what was wrong with *Lochner* is that the Court enforced the "wrong" values, a matter of a kind of judgment not uniquely possessed by judges. Brest believes, and it is hard to disagree, that "(e)ven assuming that general principles can be found in social consensus or derived by moral reasoning, the application of those principles is highly indeterminate and subject to manipulation."[17]

Brest continues, "[m]y point....is not that any of these theories are untenable, but that all are vulnerable to similar criticism based on their indeterminacy,[18] manipulability, and, ultimately, their reliance

16. 198 U. S. 45 (1905).

17. Paul Brest, "The Fundamental Rights Controversy: Essential Contradictions of Normative Constitutional Scholarship," Yale Law Journal 90 (1981), 1089.

18. The concept of "indeterminacy" has been associated with the Critical Legal Studies Movement, and Brest and this article are grouped together with that movement as an "indeterminacy" school of constitutional interpretation by Leslie Friedman Goldstein in her book, *In Defense of the Text* (Savage, Maryland: Rowman and Littlefield, 1991). She claims that adherents of this school hold that indeterminacy is a characteristic of the Constitution itself.

But the Brest article is not cited here for that proposition, as this book does *not* advance the proposition that the Constitution's meaning is always indeterminate. Nor is the claim being made here that the various theories of constitutional interpretation are of no value. On the contrary, most theories offer many useful insights. Rather, the Brest article is cited here for its correct assertion that the leading approaches to constitutional interpretation are all subject to attack, as he states, on their own terms using their own approaches. These approaches are therefore inadequate to the task which their proponents set for them: as *complete* answers to the problem of legitimacy. And the same certainly can be said of Goldstein's own unique approach.

Goldstein makes much of the controversy between "textualists or interpretivists" and "noninterpretivists," describing herself as a "moderate textualist," something she sees as very distinct from "noninterpretivists" who

on judicial value choices that cannot be 'objectively' derived from text, history, consensus, natural rights, or any other source. No theory of constitutional adjudication can defend itself against self-scrutiny."[19]

These criticisms are substantially valid and in many ways, almost obvious. Indeed, arguably, at some point, their proponents' insistence on pursuing them, despite their limitations, raises questions about their nature and value.

Interestingly, Brest ends his article by asking why constitutional scholarship is so court-centered. His answer seems to be that scholars wish to engage these questions in terms of serious, reflective moral discourse. They seek public discourse about issues of principle and ultimately shared, reflectively held public values but are skeptical about finding this anywhere else except in the work of courts, (not that courts always meet this standard). He ends by advocating that scholars join in an effort toward a genuine reconstruction of society with greater citizen participation in the community's public discourse.While this is doubtless a commendable goal for all citizens, including constitutional scholars, there may be something else for scholars in particular to pursue. Surely constitutional scholars do have a powerful need to seek and engage in discourse about issues of principle, and ultimately shared, reflectively held public values. The roots of this disposition are multiple but the tie between normative philosophy and constitutional studies is long-standing. It is in no sense disparaging of this association to point out that Brest is correct, that normative constitutional scholarship has not succeeded in defining an approach that commands general support for the simple reason that it cannot succeed.

This does not mean that the normative effort is without value but that it is not the only kind of scholarly effort of interest and value. Perhaps we might be well advised to spend more energy examining judicial activism as a phenomenon and worry a bit less about its legitimacy. It has been around for a long time and, whatever its merits, it shows no sign of disappearing.

---

believe it is appropriate to go beyond the Constitution as document to natural law, national ideals, national legal custom, or fundamental rights. Yet Goldstein's approach turns out to define textual as not simply the words of the Constitution but as properly including matters *implied* by the provisions of the document. It also covers general principles of law considered in light of both the structure of the document and the structure of the government the document sets up, and expects the judges to adapt these general principles to social changes.

19. Brest, "Fundamental Rights," 1096.

Most of the recent writing about judicial activism focuses on its legitimacy and clearly both critics and defenders of the Supreme Court are dissatisfied with existing rationales for its legitimacy. The legitimacy of judicial review, whether deemed activist or not, has always been a concern of constitutional scholars, and it is fair to say that it has been the dominant preoccupation of constitutional commentators since the court-packing crisis of the 1930s.

As Martin Shapiro has pointed out, the approach of this type of commentary has tended to be shaped by the formative experience of the commentators.[20] Most of those who experienced the crisis of the 1930s were uncomfortable with the activism of the Warren Court even though they may have shared its "liberal" views. In most instances, these commentators had been taught that the Supreme Court of the 1930s was guilty of reading its own ideological beliefs into the Constitution. The Crisis of 1936 and Settlement of 1937 had been decisive events in their intellectual formation. They could not accept easily what many saw as similar behavior by the Warren Court, and this was the case even though the Warren Court's values were in many cases similar to those of the commentators. They might applaud what the Court was doing from a policy standpoint, but they could not accept that the "means" of judicial activism was justified even by the more noble ends being pursued by the Warren Court. However, those commentators whose formative experience was during the period of Warren Court activism itself have tended to embrace it with more enthusiasm and have sought stronger rationales for its exercise, though a vocal group of dissidents have attacked it vigorously.

Certainly the exercise of extensive Supreme Court power raises significant questions in democratic and jurisprudential theory, and it is not surprising that many have found them fascinating. The widespread sense that judicial activism in the constitutional sphere was reaching a new scope and intensity in the 1950s through the 1970s made the question of legitimacy seem particularly timely and important. It may also be true that many constitutional and jurisprudential scholars simply find it hard to resist the temptation to try their own hand at resolving one of the great continuing debates of American scholarly life.

But the legitimacy of judicial activism is not the only question of scholarly importance about such activism. Indeed, given the fact that the American judiciary has been utilizing the Constitution in activist

---

20. Martin Shapiro, "Fathers and Sons: the Court, the Commentators and the Search for Values" in *The Burger Court: The Counter-Revolution that Wasn't*, Vincent Blasi, ed. (New York: Yale University Press, 1983).

ways that a significant number of contemporaries have deemed excessive for almost two hundred years, one might reasonably argue that legitimacy questions are less interesting or urgent than questions about why the practice has developed as it has. Some measure of dissatisfaction with the legitimacy of judicial activism might be relieved if activism was approached less as a philosophical problem to be solved than as a political phenomenon to be understood.

Although an occasional Supreme Court decision might make reference in its footnotes to some of this scholarly work, there is precious little evidence that most of this extensive scholarly concern has had direct and important effect on Court doctrine. If there is a connection, it is that the political conservatism of the 1980s accounts for both the attention to the extensive normative scholarly concern and the calculated appointment of reliably conservative judges. At most, the scholarship provided occasional rationalization for conservative agendas and the selection of conservative judges. Occasionally, (Robert Bork comes to mind) these writings have served as judicial campaign documents, and then, ironically, as the undoing of a campaign.

But conservative agendas and conservative judges would have been advanced by conservative presidents without any specific normative approach being set forth in the academy. Much of the normative argument that characterized the commentary of the late 1970s and 1980s has its roots in the very similar criticisms of the turn-of-the-century activist Court that led the way to the court-packing struggle of the 1930s.

Activism will inevitably and appropriately produce normative arguments that may have ideological overtones but which also make valid points. Activism always has its defenders and critics. The reason this book seeks to move beyond such argument is not because all normative criticism is to be dismissed as simply ideological or partisan but because such approaches have arguably reached a point of diminishing intellectual returns. The question of the legitimacy of judicial activism is simply no longer the most interesting question that can be asked. A broader look that considers the political-institutional context offers additional insights into the nature of the judicial activism of the Warren Court and the longevity of its principal doctrinal accomplishments.

four/ The Activism of Affirmative Remedies

Despite the preponderance of normative writing about judicial activism in the 1970s and 1980s which provided the dominant element of the intellectual context of the period, activism has sometimes been considered in relation to aspects of, or specific issues arising from, the political-institutional context. Thus, for example, the conclusions in Paul Brest's article [1] include an insightful discussion of what he calls the problem of the second best. Brest suggests that each of us holds to a fantasy that each isolated actor and action within a complex social system will reflect the system's essence, and we are skeptical about systemic justifications for acts that trouble us when looked at in isolation. He suggests an analogy with the economic theory of second best, which holds that a regulatory scheme that is inefficient when viewed in isolation may contribute to the overall efficiency of an economic system because of how it interacts with inefficiencies elsewhere in the system. He reminds us that back in 1966, Martin Shapiro[2] suggested that the"democratic" branches of government were imperfect in their democratic function and that the Court's role seemed less undemocratic and even more congruent with system objectives when the realities of the rest of the system, as opposed to theories about it, were examined.

Brest concludes that the "Madisonian dilemma," that is, a government that contains both important majoritarian and nonmajoritarian aspects, is not susceptible to resolution in its own terms. This political approach, pioneered in Shapiro's still useful work, looks

---

1. Brest, "Fundamental Rights Controversy."

2. Martin Shapiro, *Freedom of Speech* (Englewood Cliffs, N.J.: Prentice-Hall, 1966).

at the phenomenon of judicial review in relation to the other branches of government, sheds useful light on the matter by transcending the limits of increasingly circular normative debate, and looks at judicial review as a political phenomenon.

Others have examined the place of judicial review within our system in terms of the practical impact of its relationship to political majorities. Dahl's famous 1957 article (reexamined by Casper in 1976)[3] in which he argues that the extent to which the Court operates outside a dominant majority is exaggerated, is a classic example. Wallace Mendelsohn[4] argues that there is an inverse relationship between a vigorous party system and judicial activism. His argument that the Court tends to decide when decisions are not being made within the political process, whether due to extra-process "deals" like the Compromise of 1867 or because of the stalemate that is so often a product of Madisonian fragmentation and weak parties, is undoubtedly true. But the reverse is less convincing. Judicial activism, meaning the Court deciding unclear issues and stretching previous understandings about "appropriate" constitutional interpretation, has occurred at times of political deadlock and at times when the activism (in general thrust, if not in precise detail) has been supported by a strong dominant coalition. It has occurred at times of vigorous two-party competition. It is probably true that the social, cultural, and institutional conditions that characterize America have promoted both judicial activism and ineffectual party systems over much of our history. The effort to tie activism to an important element of the American political context is to be applauded, even though it is probably an oversimplification to say that eras with weak party systems give rise to periods of judicial activism.

The political-institutional phenomenon that most dramatically characterized the judicial activism of the Warren Court period in the public's mind was its emphasis on affirmative remedies. Accordingly, the nature and increased use of these remedies warrants an effort to consider it contextually.

The most famous and controversial affirmative remedy was school "busing" though, of course, when the Court held that separate but equal was inherently unequal and required that dual school systems must be

3. Robert A. Dahl, "Decision-Making in a Democracy: The Supreme Court as a National Policy-Maker," *Journal of Public Law* 6 (Fall 1957): 279; reconsidered in Jonathan A. Casper, The Supreme Court and National Policy Making,"*American Political Science Review* 60, no.1 (March, 1976): 50.

4. Wallace Mendelsohn, "The Politics of Judicial Activism," *Emory Law Journal 24* , (1975): 43.

eliminated "with all deliberate speed,"[5] large-scale urban "busing" remedies were not really apparent or foreseeable. As suggested earlier, the *Brown* decision should be understood as fundamentally an expression of the unacceptability of official, institutionalized racism. At root, *Brown* has come to mean that the state may not be used by some elements of society to impose tangible burdens on others because of their race. The use of state power by one group to isolate and stigmatize another, and to institutionalize and make "official" practice those private prejudices that still persist in our diverse society is to embark on a course of action so serious and threatening that it must be forbidden and all lingering effects of prior action eliminated.

The command to stop these practices is, in fact, well understood and broadly supported. It is the command to eliminate all vestiges of prior action and attempt to make things as they might otherwise have been--the affirmative, equitable remedy--that is far less well understood or where understood, less supported. The reasons for this are not hard to comprehend. It is one thing to tell people that they may not impose unfair burdens on others. It is another thing to tell them that they must give up something they already have or expect to have in order to compensate others for past burdens. This is particularly difficult where they do not see themselves as personally guilty; or where they may feel that, comparatively speaking, they too suffer from the effects of previous societal injustice; or where they may perceive that the process of making things as they might have otherwise been involves major amounts of speculation.

The extensive use of affirmative remedies in school desegregation cases, employment discrimination cases, and other related cases has, on the whole, proceeded as a reasoned process of expansion and development from prior decisions. But in some instances, this expansion has exceeded the consensus that supported the ending of segregation and has, to a considerable degree, opened the door for attacks upon the entire effort.

True, the results of these attacks have been strikingly uneven. Many who would temper and moderate affirmative remedies are well aware of the racism that has been harbored in American institutions in the past, as well as the role of the courts in legitimizing racism. It is hard for a court to decline to undertake to right something that is clearly wrong, indeed that has come to be seen as evil, on the grounds that the indirect effects of the remedy may do as much harm as good, or that the selective correction of some injustices may comparatively

---

5. *Brown v. Board of Education* (II), 349 U.S. 294 (1955).

worsen the feelings of unjust treatment in those whose claims to social justice are not dealt with. When the wrong is palpable, it is hard not to do something; and courts deal with racial segregation and discrimination with the only tools that they have.[6]

Still, there is no question that much of what critics associate with Warren Court activism and usually find most upsetting involves judicial imposition of affirmative remedies. It does not seem to matter that in fact many of these remedies are the result of doctrinal development at the lower federal court level and are not really directly attributable to the Supreme Court. Nor does it even seem to matter that in many instances, even when they are the result of Supreme Court activity, much of that activity actually occurred after the Warren Court had passed from the scene.

Consider the actual roots of the busing remedy. To understand busing one must first understand that it is not busing but compulsory reassignment that was the heart of most desegregation plans. This is a phenomenon that has its roots in the early experience with desegregation in southern communities, which typically had two school systems, one by law for White children, the other by law for Black children. Even if state and community authorities responded to *Brown* and repealed the laws and ordinances requiring segregated schools, announcing that from now on all schools would be open to children of both races, the chances were overwhelming that no White child in a southern town of the 1950s or early 1960s would have voluntarily transferred to a Black school. For a Black family to send their child to the all-White school would have involved serious risks. Thus years later, although the laws would be gone and the formal racial labels removed from the school, nothing fundamental would actually be different; there would still be two sets of schools, one all-Black and the other all-White. The response of the courts to this kind of situation gradually became more stringent. School districts were reminded that they must not only eliminate the laws that created segregation but also the last vestiges of the dual school system that those laws created.

---

6. "Because elected officials had created and maintained inferior schools for minority children, judges could not passively stand aside when presented with evidence of discriminatory acts. Judges felt understandably obligated to do *something*." Christopher E. Smith, *Courts and Public Policy* (Chicago: Nelson-Hall, 1993), 73.

After years of resistance, when the courts began to lose patience[7] and set deadlines, only one practical method to offer effectiveness and dispatch normally presented itself: compulsory reassignment. Courts might pair schools, ordering half the children in each to transfer to the other; or they might designate one school as exclusively for the lower grades and the other for the upper grades. Compulsory reassignment eliminated the vestiges of segregation. Busing was involved only if the distances for some children participating in the reassignment were too great. In the deep South, in some instances, integrating schools may have produced less busing than the maintenance of segregation had required. In the case of *Swann v. Charlotte Mecklenberg*[8] in 1971 (about two years after the retirement of Earl Warren from the Court), the Supreme Court summarized the development of desegregation law up to that point, emphasizing the inadequacy of "freedom of choice" plans, the obligation to eliminate dual school systems, and the appropriateness of affirmative remedies including "busing."

It was when busing came North (and West) to large multiethnic cities that it became widely identified in the public mind with danger and violence. (With few exceptions, busing in the South typically involved small- and medium-sized cities.) It was not clear for several years that busing could come North under the banner of the Constitution. Southern segregation was de jure (by law) and Northern segregation was seen as de facto (in fact)--the result of private discrimination and other nongovernmental causes. Although some argued that the government had an obligation to run public schools in a manner that overcame segregation whatever its cause, this theory never achieved legal ascendency.

Desegregation remedies involving busing became commonplace in America outside the South only after civil rights lawyers developed and established an expanded theory of de jure segregation. In many non-Southern cities with significant minority populations, a pattern of administrative actions by local government authorities could be found that supported an inference of intentional official action to segregate, or support private efforts to segregate, public schools.

Keyes v. Denver[9] offered the post-Warren Supreme Court the chance to curtail "Northern" desegregation remedies. *Denver* argued

---

7. When Congress had enacted supporting legislation strengthening federal legal initiatives, providing federal desegregation funding incentives, and providing for federal aid cutoffs for recalcitrant districts. See Chapter 5 in Rosenberg, *The Hollow Hope*.

8. 402 U.S. 1 (1971).

9. 413 U.S. 189 (1973).

that proof of official action to segregate its schools in one part of the city did not justify a city-wide busing remedy. There was no proof that all of the racial isolation in the city schools was caused by official action. Few would argue that the kind of official action to produce or support segregation that was established in the *Keyes* case and in most other Northern cases was the sole cause of racially isolated schools in *Denver* and these other cities.

Put another way, if the specific pattern of illegal official action demonstrated in these cases had never occurred, no one could seriously argue that there would have been no racial isolation in the schools of most large American cities with significant minority populations. But the Court majority accepted the argument that official segregation-producing action in one part of the school system gave rise to a presumption that it had contributed to all segregation in the system. The presumption is rebuttable, but, as a practical matter, the legal burden so created is virtually impossible to rebut. (Justice Rhenquist saw this doctrine as analogous to the medieval doctrine of "taint.")

In retrospect, it may be the case that *Keyes v. Denver*'s holding that de jure segregation in a portion of a school system created a presumption of systemwide effect was unwise. Although systemwide integration, or indeed metropolitanwide school integration, might well constitute a desirable social practice, it does not follow that it is or must be a constitutional command. The Court declined to eliminate the doctrinal distinction between de jure and de facto segregation, yet its *Keyes* doctrine had the practical result of eliminating it in many places. Admittedly, the technical problems resulting from ruling the other way--that is, holding that remedies should be limited to the portions of the system proximately impacted by the specific unconstitutional official actions or limited to the proportion of the system's racial isolation reasonably attributable to those actions--would have been formidable, but it is not clear that they would have been insurmountable.

There would be no easy way for a court to determine precisely what degree of segregation in a large urban school system was created by the demonstrated official action as compared to what degree resulted from other causes. Many would argue that since all segregation by race is wrong, a court would be wrong to try to make such a determination. Yet there was intense opposition to the citywide busing remedy and a widespread sense that in some places it has been carried too far. At the same time, there were limitations on remedy effectiveness created by the refusal, again by the post-Warren Court, in *Millikan v. Bradley*[10] to permit metropolitan remedies and eliminate suburbs as safe havens for the suburban middle class. These limitations reinforce those that arise from the ability of much of the White middle class to purchase private education for their children. Many have charged that excessive use of compulsion in urban remedies has been counterproductive, driving Whites from the public school system and thus making effective integration impossible. Others see the two cases, taken together, as creating an artificial situation that led almost automatically to citywide busing remedies while requiring the buses to screech to a stop at city lines.

The additional levels of urban integration that the *Keyes* presumption authorizes have not, in the end, been achieved in most places, and in some localities demographic changes have increased racial isolation in the public schools. What was achieved overall during the Warren and post-Warren eras, in crude and inexact fashion, was a significant level of desegregation, particularly in the South, that made credible the Warren Court's original command to refrain from and eliminate the prior effects of official, government-authorized segregation. Certainly it was necessary and appropriate to eliminate officially sanctioned dual school systems and the segregation that was directly and reasonably traceable to them. It was arguably less appropriate to seek to impose a level of integration that likely would not have existed had there never been officially supported segregation. (While many of the decisive remedy cases came after the Warren Court had technically ended, surely *Keyes* would have been decided the same way had Warren and the Warren Court justices, whose departures followed his, served for several more years. Indeed, had these justices not left, the *Millikan* case undoubtedly would have gone the other way, opening the way for judicial efforts to impose yet an additional level of integration though use of some compulsory metropolitan busing remedies.)

Stephen Halpern gives important insight into Supreme Court and lower court willingness to undertake busing and other large scale public sector equitable remedies. He suggests that the increased scope of judicial activity is "primarily attributable to the enormous growth in the scope and power of American government in the last twenty-five years." Given the "vast and virtually incomprehensible growth in the range and complexity of activities regulated by government," and our penchant to transform political issues into legal ones, our tradition and

10. 418 U.S. 717 (1974).

experience "suggest that the range of questions brought before courts will roughly correspond to the range of questions that government itself addresses."[11] He makes the shrewd point that the nature of judicial remedies has changed because the nature of the government action being challenged and voided has changed.

If one simply confronts an unconstitutional statute, it is sufficient to void it. However, where the Court's review of unconstitutional action is directed at public bureaucracies that are significantly independent from political processes, "undemocratically" organized, and largely dominant over a dependent and weak clientele, then something more is required. The public bureaucracy exercises constant and routine control through an institutional apparatus over people subject to its authority and requires them to perform affirmative behaviors. It is the nature of this administrative power to shape the nature of the judicial remedy that results when such a bureaucracy's practices are found to be unconstitutional.

An observer's perspective is further broadened when judicial activism in the constitutional arena is seen in the context of judicial activity generally. In recent years, some have attributed the growth of judicial activism in America to a new style of public interest litigation very different in scope and nature from classic litigation.[12] While there is a sense in which this may be true, it is a picture that obscures as much as it illuminates. It is based upon a comparison of the traditional small-scale two-party lawsuit with the large-scale public interest, highly complex lawsuit involving class remedies and extensive judicial supervision. It presents the latter in a manner that almost suggests it has sprung full grown from promethean, activist judges, radical lawyers, and small but determined interest groups. This is a fundamentally distorted picture for it markedly downplays, if not quite outright ignores, the enormous and largely prior growth of judicial activism in so-called private corporate legal spheres.

Bankruptcies, anti-trust, and other forms of corporate litigation are enormously complex and have been for decades. They involve judicial

---

11. Stephen Halpern, "On the Imperial Judiciary and Comparative Institutional Development and Power in America," *Supreme Court Activism and Restraint*, Stephen C. Halpern and Charles M. Lamb, eds. (Lexington, Mass.: Lexington Books, 1982), 221,223,224.

12. Most notably Abram Chayes in "The Role of the Judge in Public Law Litigation," *Harvard Law Review* 89 (1976), 1281 and "The Supreme Court 1981 Term, Foreward, Public Law Litigation and the Burger Court, " *Harvard Law Review* 96 (1982), 4.

supervision of complex institutions, representation of classes, and sweeping and detailed remedies--all of the essential features that have come to mark large-scale public interest litigation. Clearly they are the source of the public interest litigating style and doubtless too of the easy readiness of federal judges to take on the reconstruction of public institutional arrangements.

Phillip Areeda spoke of the "fearful dimensions" of many antitrust cases, and pointed to the enormous resources the government can mobilize, ranging from the hundreds of lawyers in the Antitrust Division of the Justice Department to the skills of the Federal Bureau of Investigation. Large business corporations can respond with equally major resources. In one case[13] (that went to trial in 1960, before most instances of modern public law litigation were even conceived of) according to Areeda "there were 29 defendants represented in the courtroom by about 100 attorneys. During the investigation the government had subpoenaed an estimated one million pages of documents from the defendants."[14] He also cites the government's attack on IBM's monopoly, which began in 1968 and dragged on for thirteen years. He speaks of the need for a "strong judge" to oversee this kind of litigation.

To take the best-known recent example, few Supreme Court constitutional decisions have been any more activist and sweeping than the AT&T divestiture case, which has affected all phone service customers in America.[15] The full ramifications of this case may still not be realized. Yet the public and many who inform them do not really seem to have grasped fully the scope of the tradition of such vast, massive litigation in the private corporate sphere. The very word "private" acts as a curtain to obscure sight, but there is much to see and understand if we look behind it, and most of this quite traditional judicial activity takes place at levels well below the U.S. Supreme Court.

The propensity of federal court judges to undertake the reform of local agencies should be seen as a functional extension of their routine role in the restructuring of corporations in anti-trust and bankruptcy activity. Their confidence in their capacity to handle complex

---

13 *United States v. Arkansas Fuel Oil Corp.*, 1960 Trade Cas. Section 69619 (N.D. Okla.).

14 Phillip Areeda, *Antitrust Analysis*, 3rd ed. (Boston, Mass.: Little Brown and Co., 1981), 98-99.

15. *The Deal of the Century: The Breakup of A.T.&T* by Steve Coll. (New York: Atheneum, 1986)

restructuring, their ways of dealing with varied classes of people with claims upon the institution, their notion that judicial intervention is highly appropriate to break a structural deadlock all stem from what are now long-standing judicial roles in regard to restructuring of corporations.

The truth is that judicial activism, broadly conceived, is not something that happens only to the Constitution in exceptional circumstances. It is such a regular and long-standing part of our legal and political tradition and practices that it must be seen as integral to our system.

Much of what most people have in mind when they complain about the greatest excesses of judicial activism in the 1960s and 1970s is not really Supreme Court activity at all. These people are aware of reports of courts taking over schools, prisons, and other state and local governmental institutions. They have read of sweeping judicial decrees going into the details of administration and involving court appointed masters and often expenditure of public monies. Many attribute this activity in some way to the Supreme Court whose omnipresent influence as a kind of general judicial social engineer is usually assumed.

While Supreme Court doctrine is obviously not unrelated to some of this activity, much of it is primarily the result of lower court response and innovation. That activity connected with racial, and particularly school, desegregation was in many respects and instances an arguably necessary response to *Brown* and its progeny. But some aspects of equitable remedies in these cases, and often the most controversial aspects, were not inevitable responses. And the extension of sweeping remedies to other institutions was usually not required by particular Supreme Court decisions. These remedies were within the scope of these decisions and were usually supported by the Court when challenges resulted in appellate review, but they were not really compelled by the Court or its doctrines. The development of these remedies and the disposition to use them actively primarily reflects the makeup and character of the lower federal courts in the late 1950s, 1960's, and early 1970s--(a character that has been significantly and purposefully changed in the 1980s). And the judgment--positive, negative, or mixed--upon this activity is properly a judgment upon these men and their work; it does not really belong primarily at the doorstep of Earl Warren and the Supreme Court.[16]

---

16. A number of much-publicized activist thrusts have also been initiated by state supreme courts. The most significant area of activity has been in school finance with holdings that the traditional method of heavy reliance on local property taxes violates the state constitution's requirements of equality

Much of the effort to achieve school (and other) desegregation in the deep South was the result of vigorous and often creative legal activity by four judges of the Fifth Circuit Court of Appeals during the critical years of the 1960s: John Minor Wisdom, Elbert Tuttle, Richard Taylor Rives, and John R. Brown. And many are aware of the immeasurable influence of District Court Judge Frank A. Johnson, a virtual one-man judicial army whose federal court asserted jurisdiction during a period of about fifteen years over the property tax assessment program, prisons, mental health agency public education system and highway patrol of Alabama.[17]

While lower court activism has not received the attention that the Supreme Court's has, it has been investigated by some scholars. Phillip J. Cooper considers several lower court cases involving subjects including public housing, prisons, mental health facilities, and school desegregation. Cooper concludes that arguments about whether or not judges should or should not become involved in such cases ignore the reality of the situation they confront. "They simply are not in a position to refuse to respond to proper cases instituted by appropriate parties under provisions of statutory or constitutional law."[18]

Certainly this is truer than many critics would like to admit, though it may also be true that there is somewhat greater judicial choice as to the specific nature and scope of involvement than some have considered. Questions of long-term efficacy may prompt greater attention and sensitivity to that issue in the future.

When the efficacy of these remedies is systematically considered, the results of the intervention are usually deemed to be problematic because of successful resistance by the bureaucracies involved.[19] The

---

given the wide disparity of tax bases within school districts. Thus even though the U.S. Supreme Court rejected such a claim when brought under the federal constitution by a 5-4 vote in *San Antonio Independent School District v. Rodriquez*, 411 U.S. 1 (1973), several states including California, Texas, and New Jersey have had to develop plans to provide compensatory, equalizing funding for schools in less affluent areas.

17. Jack Bass, *Unlikely Heroes* (New York: Simon and Schuster, 1981).

18. Phillip J. Cooper, *Hard Judicial Choices: Federal District Court Judges and State and Local Officials* (New York: Oxford University Press, 1988), 328.

19. Robert Wood, *Remedial Law* (Amherst, Mass.: University of Massachusetts Press, 1990). This book is based upon a symposium held at Wesleyan University. Most of the symposium members had participated earlier in prominent cases involving broad equitable remedies directed against public institutions. Given the tenor of the book, it might well have been subtitled, "the legal process meets the real world of public administration."

desire for autonomy and resistance to change, which are traits of all organizations are strikingly evident in public bureaucracies. Organizations resist because their members will always make contradictory judgments as to whether change is necessary; ineffective decision-making processes may prevail, and external instructions may seem impractical or ambiguous.

Public bureaucracies lack the clear private standard--profit--by which to measure achievement. Also, public bureaucracies tend to be the constant recipients of "double-bind" messages because the nature of most politics is to avoid sharp conflict and confrontation and to promote the blurring of disagreement by agreeing with all sides. In response to such cross-pressures, legislatures will frequently enact mandates for public agencies that are blatantly contradictory, passing the contradictions on to the "bureaucrats" to worry about.

For a bureaucracy, the result of such endless contradictory messages and conflicting cross-pressures can indeed be a powerful institutional search for autonomy and avoidance of accountability to outside forces, a rigid resistance to change, and at some point, even a kind of institutional nervous breakdown where nothing really works at all. An institution like this will certainly fail to secure the constitutional rights of those it is supposed to protect, and it may well appear to a court like a bankrupt institution: morally, constitutionally, and perhaps financially too. But such "bankruptcies" can involve institutional pathologies far greater and more complex than may be involved in private bankruptcies and the quagmire that awaits judicial intervention may consequently prove to be more immense.

Where the critics of lower court activism working toward reforming public agencies might properly focus their efforts is not upon the newness or even the arrogance of such judicial activism, but rather on its efficacy. The question of democratic accountability is, of course, potentially an issue. However, seeing judicial intervention as always undemocratic, and bureaucratic practice as always the result of strict adherence to democratic accountability, lacks some appreciation for the realities of government. The resistance of some bureaucracies to public control is legendary. Indeed, close study of some famous instances of judicial intervention suggests that such intervention is sometimes sought by some elements of a bureaucracy as a means of further insulating it from, or strengthening its hand in, struggles with other "democratic" institutions.

Where courts have intervened, it has not usually been to frustrate policies that have been formulated in some reasonably clear-cut democratic manner. The more practical problem has been that public bureaucracies do not operate just like corporate bureaucracies,[20] and the environment in which they operate differs from that in which corporate bureaucracies operate in numerous critical ways. Many judicial methods, techniques, and approaches, tried and true when directed to corporations, prove less effective in the public sector. As a result, courts have often found their interventions into public agency restructuring frustrating and arguably even counterproductive experiences.

Put another way, it is the complex, arcane, and even perverse and irrational nature of "real" politics, rather than the precepts of democratic theory, that is the greater obstacle to successful lower court activism and the continued fashioning of sweeping affirmative remedies in the public sector. While there have certainly been some real accomplishments, it is the ambiguous nature of their overall experiences as much as the recent changes in the ideological makeup of lower federal court judges that will likely provoke a long-run tendency toward greater judicial restraint in this area in the future.[21]

Examining the kinds of political and institutional considerations that surround the activism of affirmative remedies offers much of interest. But it does not do much to link judicial activism with developments in the broader society. One notable political approach that does move analysis in this direction might be described as neo-Marxist.[22] This approach often suggests that what the Court has done since the 1930s is fundamentally conservative in that it is designed to make corporate capitalism rational through a kind of elitist social engineering that centralizes on behalf of a national economy, that it provides only symbolic and illusory liberty and equality to enhance social control and, insofar as it achieved any real change, that it did so

---

20. Of course, private bureaucracies do not always operate like private bureaucracies either. See Herbert Simon, *Administrative Behavior* (New York: Macmillan, 1947) for an argument that private bureaucracies will sometimes sacrifice profit for "satisficing."

21. On the frustrations of lower court activism, see Stephen C. Halpern, *On the Limits of the Law: The Ironic Legacy of Title VI of the 1964 Civil Rights Act* (Baltimore: Johns Hopkins University Press, 1994); R. Shep Melnick, *Regulation and the Courts: The Case of the Clean Air Act* (Washington,D.C.: Brookings Institution, 1983); Donald Horowitz, *The Courts and Social Policy* (Washington, D.C.: Brookings Institution, 1977).

22. A representative example of the genre is Joan Roelofs, "Judicial Activism as Social Engineering: A Marxist Interpretation of the Warren Court,"in *Supreme Court Activism and Restraint,* Stephen C. Halpern and Charles M. Lamb, eds. (Lexington, Mass.: Lexington Books, 1982), 249.

to ward off more radical change in the Cold War era. This approach also argues that the Court activity was part of a broader elite effort to depoliticize the mass of the population by excluding some important questions from the public realm.

While this type of political-institutional approach, which does suggest that Court activity is connected to broader developing social and economic factors, has some strongly positive aspects to it, it tends to be overwhelmed by the simplistic reductionism of other parts. The implication that Court-activated reforms are somehow arranged--it is never really clear by whom--as part of a calculated effort to ward off the otherwise imminent "real" change, never makes very clear just what this radical alternative would look like and what the basis is for suggesting that such options were in any sense realistically available (never mind desirable). And to describe the Court as an agent of elite manipulation and its activities as increasing "depoliticization" may confuse an association for a causal relationship.

The kind of democratization and expansion of rights that we have seen in America in this century has indeed been associated in the broadest sense with the requirements of the economic system. It may not be appreciated that there is a sense in which the enjoyment and exercise of some traditional rights have aspects to them that resemble what economists call positional goods.[23] This means that at least part of their value to individuals and groups in the past may have been due to the fact that only a limited number of people enjoyed them. When much larger numbers of people acquire them and they are enjoyed by a mass middle class, certain sorts of traditional legal and political struggles associated with their maintenance may come to seem too wasteful of time and money for most of its members to want to engage in on a routine basis. These "practical" people want to have the kinds of political and social relationships that the Court has nationalized and set standards for, predictably and reliably available to them without being subject to the vagaries of routine local electoral politics. And the Court's activities may be seen as responsive to this demand.

But describing this response as depoliticization is certainly debatable. That elite hegemony somehow acts to depoliticize the American political system to keep it from grappling with certain kinds of issues is a venerable claim. Walter Dean Burnham has claimed that the system "disaggregates."[24] And even Justice Felix Frankfurter

---

23. See Fred Hirsch, *Social Limits to Growth* (Cambridge: Harvard University Press, 1977).

24. See Walter Dean Burnham, *Critical Elections and the Mainsprings of American Politics* (New York, W. W. Norton, 1970).

frequently argued that Supreme Court activism on civil liberties undermined a democratic concern for these issues by encouraging people to believe that the Supreme Court would take care of them.

There may well be some force to all these arguments. Nevertheless, it cannot be disputed that the Supreme Court after 1937, while moving with increasing energy into civil liberties issues, simultaneously moved out of the vast arena of economic and social policy and returned it to the elected branches. Certainly this is the opposite of depoliticizing. A large part of the Court's civil liberties and civil rights activism was successfully designed to promote political activity, permit dissident speech, protect voting, and end malapportionment of legislatures; it cannot even be debatably characterized as "depoliticizing." Thus, even conceding that much criticism of the American political system as being depoliticized and disaggregated may be valid, it really does seem to be stretching things to conclude that Warren Court activism, when taken as a whole, can be fairly faulted as having contributed to depoliticization in America.

Perhaps the most interesting work on the Supreme Court of recent years is Gerald Rosenberg's *The Hollow Hope*. The evident purpose of the book is to establish that a perceived widespread view of the Supreme Court as the major progenitor of social change--what he terms the Dynamic Court view--is unjustified. Since the view is something of a straw man, unsurprisingly, Rosenberg has little difficulty in demolishing it. Most valuable is his extensive marshaling of evidence of underlying political, economic, and demographic changes in both the race relations and gender areas in support of his correlative claim that the social change that has ultimately resulted in areas commonly credited to the Court has its real roots in these broader developments. On the other hand, one does not have to adopt all of the accoutrements and premises of contemporary cultural studies to suggest that the symbolic impact of *Brown* may not lend itself to hard statistical measurement. As mentioned in the previous chapter, the relationship of *Brown* to the rest of its intellectual-cultural context, and the relationship of that context to political and societal developments, is difficult to measure. There is an interaction between judicial doctrine and societal change in the areas Rosenberg explores that is arguably understated by focusing on demolishing a view of the Court as prime instigator of change.

All of the political-institutional approaches to the problem of judicial review that have been discussed in this chapter are valuable because they go beyond simply considering the rightness or wrongness of activist judicial review. But many do not go far enough because they are still, in a sense, too court-centered. The most valuable approaches make an effort to look at judicial review and judicial activism within the broader context of its historical development and societal functioning. Attempting to understand it in this way illuminates how it has functioned and when such functioning has been successful and unsuccessful. The resulting insights are both more interesting and more satisfying than narrower efforts. Certainly judicial activism in the constitutional sphere seems less irregular when the observer's perspective is broadened as Brest's or Shapiro's or Halperin's or Rosenberg's efforts have already illustrated. Broadening the approach still further can be expected to yield additional understanding.

five/ The Tradition of Creative Constitutional Development

Judicial activism is a form of creative constitutional development. The practice of making "creative" or "useful" constitutional adjustments of dubious formal legitimacy has been a characteristic of the British and American constitutional systems for centuries. The tendency in America to engage in this practice is not limited to the judiciary but has become focused there because of the Supreme Court's claim to constitutional supremacy. Indeed at some place in our political system, efforts at creative constitutional development are always going on.

Judicial review is sometimes described as one of the most significant American contributions to government. That the institution is widely appreciated is demonstrated by its adoption, in one form or another, by several countries around the world since World War II (and not only in countries we occupied after the war). This appreciation may be traced in part to the prestige of the Warren Court and the perception of its critical role in fostering the civil rights revolution of the 1950s and 1960s. But it is also due to a broader recognition of the American Supreme Court's role as the vindicator of civil liberties and the sense that the Court helps keep the Constitution a real force and a relevant presence in our political affairs.

That the Court's doing this also means, in some sense, adapting the Constitution to changing circumstances is also perceived. Judicial review has long been controversial for many reasons, but the primary one is that defending the Constitution through review of arguably unconstitutional legislation is rarely achieved without simultaneously developing the Constitution, which usually expands it, or sometimes shrinks it, but almost always in important cases, changes its previously understood scope or meaning.

Some find significance in a distinction between "interpretive" and "noninterpretive" review, usually drawing a distinction between subjects explicitly mentioned in the Constitution and those inferred. This distinction serves some people's sense of the proper, but it has little practical value. If protecting speech is all right because speech is explicitly mentioned in the document, but protecting expressive action is not appropriate, because it is not mentioned, what do we do with a political opinion expressed to or by a deaf person through sign language? Is saying that speech infers communication through gestures really all that different from saying that the Fourth and Fifth Amendments infer a right of privacy? After all, protection against unreasonable search and seizure is traditionally explained with the old saying that "a man's home is his castle and not even the King of England may enter without a warrant." And the Fifth Amendment's guarantee against self-incrimination is usually explained in terms of the dignity of the individual person and as a protection against torture and other coercive methods that affront individual dignity.

The constitutional doctrine that has developed around the unmentioned right of privacy has led to issues that divide many Americans. And much sport is made, by some of those enamored of the interpretive-noninterpretive distinction, of Justice Douglas's "penumbras" and "emanations" in the *Griswold* case. But in fact, his underlying argument that there are powerful implications of privacy in the First, Fourth, and Fifth Amendments strikes many thoughtful Americans as only common sense, as Judge Bork discovered at his unsuccessful confirmation hearings. There is also the problem of the Ninth Amendment, which can be explained away only by ignoring its rather plain words.

Many speak of the Court as if its "proper" and noncontroversial role is to patrol the limits set by the Constitution.[1] They imply then, that the controversy centers on something else: the appropriateness of interpretation--a different process which goes beyond mere patrolling.

---

1. "The function of the Court was to patrol the constitutional boundaries of the other branches (the legislature especially) and of the states and keep them within their prescribed limits. The purpose of an independent judiciary was to insure that the limited and supreme Constitution remained so" Gary L. McDowell, "A Modest Remedy for Judicial Activism," *Public Interest*, no. 67 (1982) as quoted in William Lasser, *The Limits of Judicial Power* (Chapel Hill, University of North Carolina Press, 1988).

It is, above all, the proper scope of this interpretive function, this going beyond straightforward boundary patrol, that is at issue.

But this distinction is largely mythic. Certainly in recent decades, one would have to scour the reports to find a case of any significance that involves a "simple" matter of Supreme Court "boundary patrol." Normal judicial review *is* constitutional interpretation and normal constitutional interpretation involves constitutional development. It routinely involves changing what was previously understood about the Constitution. Cases that do not involve this aspect are the deviant cases, not the norm.

It seems insufficiently emphasized that the American legal-political-constitutional system is derived from a British tradition of organic evolution marked by continuous attempts to adjust existing arrangements to changing circumstances while maintaining the form of the arrangements. According to Richard Neely, "the whole body of legal rules and precedents which we call constitutional law can make sense only if . . . we conceive of a constitution not only as a document but as a set of remembered experiences occurring, in the case of this country, from the Norman conquest until today." Neely sees judicial power as a necessary mechanism for adjusting American political practice to its mythology. He sees constitutional law as "no more theoretical than plumbing"; as "generated by practical men in response to practical problems." He also believes that "law is more a function of the attitudes of the judges than of a set of principles which are understood, although . . . by a complex psychological process, law is frequently a function of a set of principles which are *not* understood."

Neely argues that we do not "have one man-one vote on most of the crucial issues of society's survival and never have had. What we have is a rule of law growing out of a nine-hundred-year Anglo-American tradition that gives us a total process of institutional balance of which one man, one vote is an integral part. What is called 'American Democracy' is really remarkable for its non-democracy, that is, its protection of minorities, dissenters, incompetents, and social outcasts."[2]

Certainly the British political system has undergone drastic changes since, say, the seventeenth-century accession of William and Mary. Yet, as has been often pointed out, an examination of the written documents that are the constituents of, or nominally reflect, the British constitution will tell one very little of its actual substantive workings today. This process of change came to pass in ways that no one would

---

2. Richard Neely, *How the Courts Govern America* (New Haven:, Conn. Yale University Press, 1981): 17.

confuse with the American process of judicial review but that nevertheless involves two parallels with that institution.

One is the conserving style of constitutional change. In Britain, the written provisions and the governmental forms that they require remain, but understandings have developed that dramatically alter the substance of the political relationship described or prescribed by the written documents. In America, the written provisions of the original Constitution largely remain but are supplemented by an interpretive doctrine, derived from hundreds of opinions, that is so substantive that it adds dimensions to the written document doubtless undreamt of by its authors.

The British practice is "old wine in new bottles" and the fact that the forms no longer encompass the old substance is now generally understood.[3] In America, it is a principle generally insisted upon that the old substance is not gone--that it is only adapted to modern circumstances through interpretation that is at most a kind of supplemental additive. Yet, if you add enough new ingredients to old wine, it may ultimately be as new as if you poured out the old and poured in an entirely new wine.

A second parallel is that the leadership of the creative constitutional development process had a quality that could be described as nondemocratic. In Britain, a sociopolitical elite carried out the process operating largely through Parliament. In America, constitutional development has become the exclusive province of the appointed Supreme Court.

This has not happened because other institutions of American government have not tried to get involved, of course. There have been many instances of the Congress or, more frequently, the president engaging in what might be seen as efforts to foster constitutional development. State governments have engaged in it too.

Many of the best-known examples of creative constitutional development occurred early in our history and involved the growth of political parties, presidential nominating conventions, and the winner-take-all electoral vote system with electors pledged to vote for their party's candidate. Other later examples include the two-term presidential tradition that FDR broke, which was then restored by a constitutional amendment; and the practice of malapportioning state legislatures and congressional districts, which prevailed until the Supreme Court changed course in the 1960s.

---

3. See generally, Walter Badgehot, *The English Constitution* (Ithaca, N.Y.: Cornell University Press, 1966).

In the recent period, one might mention the assumption of presidential power to unilaterally commit troops to foreign military objectives, such as President Bush assumed in Panama. Similarly, one could point to the passage by Congress of any number of pieces of legislation in the face of previous Supreme Court decisions, which, if adhered to, would make the legislation unconstitutional. President Nixon unsuccessfully attempted a bit of constitutional development when he suggested, during the Watergate tapes dispute, that the president might not have to follow a Supreme Court decision about presidential powers that was not "definitive," which probably meant a majority against him but a significant minority on his side.[4]

All of this, in a sense, reflects efforts to develop the American Constitution, many of which were successful--at least for a period of time. But the reason why such activity by the elected institutions of American government is not usually seen for what it is, is that in America, it cannot be fully and finally legitimate from a constitutional standpoint because of the general acceptance of the Supreme Court's first instance of creative constitutional development--the one in which it asserted and took for itself the final and exclusive prerogative to say what the Constitution means.

Because the Court's claim is exclusive, the actions of other governmental institutions in developing the Constitution, no matter how widely supported and long-standing, cannot be fully legitimate unless and until the Supreme Court ratifies them. If the Supreme Court lacked this power, or more precisely, if its claim had not become accepted, then at least some of these nonjudicial examples of creative constitutional development might have become fully accepted as permanent parts of the Constitution with the passage of time. Where the Court is most hesitant, for example, its reluctance to confront the president's war-making power, such claims by the president come closest to achieving true legitimacy.

Vigorous activity by the Court in developing the Constitution is likely to be attacked as judicial activism and the criticism is frequently presented as a defense of democracy and the collateral obligation of judicial deference to elected legislatures. But to gain some further understanding of the matter, we must try to distinguish between hostility to activist constitutional development as carried on by the judiciary and hostility to creative constitutional development as such.

---

4. If the recent use of the filibuster to block routine parts of the President's program persists, it might well be viewed as an effort at creative constitutional development.

To a constitutional "fundamentalist," judicial activism is bad because under the guise of protecting the Constitution, it actually attacks true constitutional legitimacy, the source of which is certain extraordinary majorities of the past and their understandings of and intentions regarding the provisions they embedded in the Constitution. Anger of critics is then focused upon a judiciary that is seen as violating those understandings. But if we had no tradition of judicial review and it was congressional majorities that were violating these understandings in the same way, presumably the anger of the critics would also be the same (or at least, almost the same).

For example, a fundamentalist like Raoul Berger rejects the idea that the first section of the Fourteenth Amendment has anything to do with voting.[5] And although he believes the Amendment was intended to be enforced by the Congress and not the Court, he would still, presumably, reject the idea that Congress through the fifth section can enforce the first section to expand suffrage rights. If the elected Congress or the elected President engage in constitutional activism by going beyond the intention of the extraordinary majority that enacted a constitutional provision, then these branches too are, to a fundamentalist, behaving improperly.

Superficially, it seems worse for an unelected court of nine people appointed for life to be "creatively" developing the Constitution; it suggests undemocratic rule by a group of Platonic philosopher-kings. And it is indeed sometimes the case that judicial activism which supports creative constitutional development by other elected branches may be less criticized. Nevertheless, if the essence of constitutional legitimacy is seen as giving strict respect to an action of an extraordinary majority and the intent that surrounded it, then subsequent action in conflict with that intent by an ordinary majority is illegitimate. After all, the whole point of requiring extraordinary majorities to amend the Constitution is to put something beyond the reach of an ordinary "democratic" majority.

Therefore it is the activism itself, that is, the "creative constitutional development," and not the fact that it is coming from an

---

5. Raoul Berger, *Government by Judiciary*, (Cambridge,Mass: Harvard University Press, 1977) page 7. "In short, the proof is almost incontrovertible that the framers meant to leave control of suffrage with the States, which had always exercised such control, and to exclude federal intrusion." He also cites favorably Justice Harlan's opinion in *Oregon v. Mitchell*, 400 U.S. 112, 200 (1970) where Harlan says "...there is virtually unanimous agreement, clearly and repeatedly expressed, that Section 1 of the Amendment did not reach discriminatory voter disqualifications."

unelected judiciary, that is the core of the real offense to the fundamentalist critics of judicial activism. And illegitimate constitutional development cannot be made truly legitimate to a fundamentalist by obtaining a congressional majority or 51 percent in a Gallop Poll.

Yet, as mentioned, there is in fact a long-standing British and American practice of creatively developing, often dramatically, substantive constitutional arrangements while maintaining the original forms or provisions. The tradition is venerable, often associated with conservative societal forces and historically, it is by no means simply or primarily associated with instances of tyranny or abuse of power, though it sometimes has been. Paradoxically, although carried on by processes that can be criticized as undemocratic or non-democratic, it has often, though not invariably, been associated with what many historians have later concluded was the opposite--with expanded liberty, with strengthened constitutionalism, with expanded democratic political participation and with compassionate concern for social welfare. It is truly a matter filled with ambiguity.

Consider too that clear-cut constitutional change occurs in two ways. One is by means of constitutional amendment through the prescribed formal processes; the other is through successful revolution--the use of force that is acceded to. The American Constitution has not experienced change by force except that which grew out of the Civil War. The Civil War itself was, of course, a kind of attempted revolution and the North's victory settled the debated constitutional point about the nature of the union. Revolution was the only way the South could have successfully prevailed on their theory of the Constitution; they lacked an amending majority.

By the same token, the North's imposition of their point of view about the nature of the Union was achieved by the force of arms of their victorious army, and was in a sense revolutionary. They too lacked an amending majority. The amendments the radical republicans added to the Constitution were ratified, in many instances, at virtual gunpoint. The Supreme Court declined to give weight to challenges to this process, however, giving deference to the view of the (truncated) Congress that the amendments had in fact been ratified. Put another way, they were not inclined to permit the re-fighting of the Civil War in Court. (Interestingly enough, the Congress never did add an amendment prohibiting a state from withdrawing from the Union; presumably, they deemed it superfluous in light of the war's outcome.)

The other clear-cut way to change the American Constitution is through amendment. After the addition of the Bill of Rights shortly after ratification, the Constitution has seen only seventeen successful formal amendments. Yet no one would argue that the Constitution has changed in only these seventeen ways in two hundred years. The Constitution, or at least our valid understanding of what it requires, has been altered in numerous fundamental ways over two hundred years through a process of "creative" constitutional development.

Creative constitutional development is a basic part of the American political tradition. It is also an important British tradition. And although understandably, there have always been people who looked askance upon instances of its execution, it has frequently been resorted to in both countries and has often with sometime surprising speed been acceded to as legitimate. In part that is because America and Britain have had, at least since the time of Cromwell, genuine revolutionary traditions to which the creative constitutional development process has been linked. To put it another way, it simply looks less irregular to see the Constitution "developed" instead of formally amended when one is aware that revolution is the other clear cut way in which the British and American Constitutions have been changed.

In England, since English judges operated from the beginning as magistrates (something like deputy kings), the distinction between law and constitutional law under conditions of strong monarchy was not clear-cut. Although Parliamentary supremacy limits the scope of British judges in the modern era, the American judiciary adopted early on both the creative traditions of the common law and the accompanying sense of magistrate's prerogative, and it has manifested no serious disposition to avoid similar practices in the area of constitutional law.[6]

Creative interpretations of Edward Coke are notable in the development of the English tradition. Although his most audacious effort, the attempt to utilize the common law to control king and Parliament never took root in England, it rooted well in America where

---

6. "Thirteenth century critics, for example, claimed that the judiciary was less active under good King Edward the Confessor, a pre-Norman king noted for his morality and justice, who allegedly left the administration of justice to the landlords. The authority for this view came from an alleged collection of laws which were usually referred to as the *Lex Edwardi Confessoris.* These purported laws of the earlier period did not exist in any coherent, consistent written form, and never had existed except in the imagination of dissatisfied litigants, until the judges turned the whole idea to their own use and began spouting new law based on the supposed *Lex Edwardi.*" Neely, *How the Courts Govern,* 41.

the existence of a written document gave an appearance of concreteness to exercise of such judicial power. Control by principles of the common law or natural law or natural justice lack the concreteness of control by a democratically adopted written constitution, even if the Court today has come to be seen by many as doing little more than reading its own notions of natural right into the document.

The very accession of William and Mary, which validated parliamentary supremacy and constitutional monarchy in Britain was technically unconstitutional as matters were then understood. The entire "glorious" process was surrounded by creative constitutional fictions that gained acceptance. And the evolution of democratically accountable executive power in Britain, as discussed in the work of Badgehot and others, is well known in its creativity. It is perhaps best symbolized by the fiction of the Queen giving the speech from the throne to Parliament each year setting forth what her government is going to do. The constitutional reality is, of course, that the speech is written for her by the prime minister and she must read it word for word. If there is an election between two speeches and the other party wins, the Queen may sound like a staunch conservative one year and a flaming socialist the next.

The disposition to be constitutionally creative was strong in North America. The colonists undertook a revolution on behalf of some creative constitutional notions about their proper role in relation to the British government. They then drafted their own governing documents: state constitutions and the Articles of Confederation.

There is no little irony in the fact that the document we call the Constitution itself emerged as a major act of creative constitutional development. After all, the mandate of the convention that drafted it was just to propose amendments to the Articles of Confederation. The delegates chose to disregard this mandate; they wrote a new Constitution with built-in ratification devices and pushed it through to adoption regardless of technical proprieties. The American Constitution was literally born in a process of creative constitutional development that disregarded existing constitutional understandings and legitimacy.

There is also no little irony in conservatives who are highly critical of activist development, celebrating a Constitution for both the nobility of its founding and its longevity without taking due note both of the fact that it was born in an act of creative development of dubious formal legitimacy, and of the likelihood that the activism that makes it a "living" document may help account for its longevity.

The Civil War period was one marked by extraordinary constitutional creativity, and President Abraham Lincoln was perhaps the principal activist during that period. On the subject of Lincoln's activity, Sanford Levinson's book, *Constitutional Faith* quotes the nineteenth-century diarist, George Templeton Strong, to the effect that while "subordination of government to the Constitution and to law is good--very good--among the best things," but "it's not the only good thing. To save the country is also good." Strong goes on to point out that it was "an object of some public importance" to prevent "Jeff Davis from chasing Lincoln out of Washington in 1861" and that this objective was such as "to justify a little unconstitutionality." Strong suggests that "[r]espect for written law and constitutions may be excessive and no less deadly than hypertrophy of the heart." A nation that becomes "finally crystallized into permanent, definite form and . . . incapable of developing new organs or agencies to meet new conditions is *dead* [; it] will begin to decompose whenever time brings the new conditions." [7]

The ways in which Lincoln, the Civil War, and the decade that followed developed and changed previous constitutional arrangements, and understandings were numerous and extensive. The three enacted constitutional amendments were only a small part of the process of development, and arguably it was the Congress and the Executive Branch, not the Supreme Court, that initiated the most significant actions. (Certainly too, the coercive methods utilized to achieve ratification of the three amendments, particularly the Fourteenth Amendment, were quite novel to say the least.)

The Compromise of 1876 was, of course, a nonjudicial and largely informal constitutional settlement that began a process that developed the then recently amended Constitution in ways that undermined much of what Reconstruction Congresses thought they were accomplishing. That process led to the rise of Jim Crow, and the Supreme Court ratified these developments. Overall, this was a very major instance of activist constitutional development, only part of which was judicial, and it is one that lasted for decades into the midtwentieth century until the Compromise and much of the ratifying judicial doctrine were undone.

At least a portion of the attempt by the Court to block state and federal regulation of the important aspects of the evolving national industrial economy also may be seen as creative constitutional development. The extent of congressional regulatory power was not

---

7. Sanford Levinson, *Constitutional Faith*,(Princeton, New Jersey: Princeton University Press, 1988), 141-142 quoting *The Diary of George Templeton Strong*, Volume 4, Allen Nevins and Milton H. Thomas, eds. (New York: Macmillan, 1952), 20-21 (entry of July 15, 1865).

definitively settled and thus, subject to legitimate disagreement, but certainly *Lochner v. New York*[8] was creative development limiting previously available state power, and of course, it was ultimately set aside as part of a great struggle that led to further development in different directions.

The struggle over whether the national government possessed the full power to promote and regulate a national economy, which culminated in the Court-packing crisis, produced a decisive victory for those who favored such governmental power. The victory was so decisive that it too can be viewed as a kind of "settlement" with both conservatives and liberals supporting it from the mid-1930s to the present day. And few people would challenge the conclusion that the victory was necessary even where they might quarrel with some specific resultant regulatory policies.

The settlement was seen as a necessary response to the exigencies of the Great Depression and necessary too to permit the emergence of modern America. Most significantly, Supreme Court decisions from *NLRB v. Jones and Laughlin Steel Corporation*[9] through *Wickard v. Filburn*[10] established a broad and sweeping view of Congress's Interstate Commerce power with little if any practical limits in the economic arena.

And although it can be plausibly argued that such a result is inherent in the Commerce power, and that it is not the Constitution that was changed but rather commerce and the nature of the economy that changed over a two hundred year period, it is indisputable that the new conception of interstate commerce altered previous understandings of where national power ended and indeed, the prior belief that there had to be some significant aspects of intrastate commerce that the national government could not reach.

Since it ratified legislation enacted by the elected branches of government, the rationale of, say, *Wickard* is not usually described as judicial activism. It is *Carter v. Carter Coal*[11] and its numerous predecessors that are described as stubborn judicial activism because they were seen as frustrating congressional (and presidential) intent and thereby, the will of the people.

But the pronouncement of doctrine that creates (or confirms and legitimizes) powers that were not generally understood to have previously existed is certainly judicial activism. As an understanding of

8. 198 U.S. 45 (1905).
9. 301 U.S. 1 (1937).
10. 317 U.S. 111 (1942).
11. 298 U.S. 238 (1936).

what the Constitution permitted or did not permit, it was invented and imposed even if it was done with the consent of (really, the insistence of) the elected branches. This mandate of majoritarian democracy may seem to make the activism of *Wickard v. Filburn* more legitimate, but does it? A true constitutional fundamentalist would say that if it was necessary to amend the Constitution in the 1930s, then the way to amend it was to amend it. A majority of Congress, a president, and a Supreme Court majority do not add up to a constitutional amending majority. (After all, if Roosevelt could have achieved enactment of a constitutional amendment, he would have taken that route. He did what he did, even to trying to pack the Court, because he could not amend.)

The constitutional test for the congressional interstate commerce power (and other powers) that emerged resulted in a national regulatory authority broad enough to carry all of the New Deal on its back and support anything that Congress had done or might need to do. These tests simply were not understood to prevail previously. The new constitutional doctrine came about and was supported because it was believed to be necessary. It has lasted because that belief was validated by subsequent experience. Modern America needed a national economy, national regulation, and a Constitution that responded to those needs, and that is what the Supreme Court gave it in the "constitutional settlement of 1937." The Constitution was not amended --could not have been amended; the Constitution was "developed."

The Constitution makes the president commander-in-chief and gives the Congress the power to declare war. Events prior and subsequent to the Second World War have resulted in the development of the "imperial presidency" in the area of national security. On the whole, these developments have been acceded to by the Congress, the Court, and the American people, though the final chapter on this dramatic example of creative constitutional development has yet to be written.

All of the examples that have been set forth here and many others that could be listed are well known and much written about individually and uniquely. But such perspectives suggest that they are in some sense deviant. The claim here is that they are not, that "creative constitutional development" is as American (and British) as apple pie (kidney pie?). However, there has not been much commentary that deals systematically with the phenomenon of creative constitutional development within the British or American political systems.

One notable effort is the work of Bruce Ackerman.[12] He has taken three significant American events--the Founding, Reconstruction, and the New Deal--and tried to legitimize the latter two by arguing that they constitute a new, non-Article 5 way of amending the Constitution, which involves certain interactions among the branches of government at the national level but that minimizes or eliminates the role of the states. It is legitimate, he says, because the process emerges from actors who could properly claim to speak for "We the People" as constitutional majority.

This approach is seen as negating the claims of constitutional fundamentalists since under it, Article 5 amendments are no longer the only way to amend the Constitution. Reasoning from this initial leap, Ackerman suggests that the Court, then, is not undemocratically activist in many of its most controversial decisions. He says it is merely recognizing in these decisions what some of its critics do not, that the Constitution has been amended without amendments and that these non-Article 5 amendments have to be worked into our constitutional law.

But while much of Ackerman's work is extremely interesting, it does not really convince. It is undoubtedly true, as he says, that the Reconstruction amendments were adopted by methods that were irregular by prior understandings. But these methods were also irregular by most subsequent understandings too. Whether or not an instance of creative constitutional development is an expression of "We the People" really depends on whether it prevails over time. Were a current president to use the army to dissolve state legislatures that refuse to ratify say, the currently proposed balanced budget amendment, the action would not, one presumes, be seen as expressing the sentiments of "We the People." But the Fourteenth Amendment was ratified less because the Reconstruction Congress somehow spoke for "We the People" than because it effectively commanded the army that won the Civil War and occupied the South. Had the South occupied the North, the voice of "We the People" might have had a different accent. Was the "Compromise of 1876," which contradicted much of what Ackerman says "We the People" did in the 1860s, any less an expression of "We the People's" views? If we tried to answer that

---

12. Bruce Ackerman, "Constitutional Politics/Constitutional Law," *Yale Law Journal* 99 1989): 453. Ackerman develops his views more elaborately in two books of what is ultimately intended to be a three book series. *We the People,* Volume 1, Foundations (Cambridge, Mass.: Harvard University Press, 1991) and *We the People,* Volume 2, Transformations (Cambridge, Mass.: Harvard University Press, 1998).

question at any time from the 1880s through the 1940s we would probably have had to say "no."

The New Deal's changes were radical indeed and, as Ackerman claims, certainly were not simply restoration. But the Settlement of 1937 developments were not the first changes to the Constitution without benefit of amendment and there will probably be others. The changes had less to do with "We the People" speaking through a new method of non-Article 5 amendment than with the failure of one attempt at constitutional development, epitomized by *Lochner,* and its replacement by another.

To say that the undoubtedly nationalist Settlement of 1937 provided the "amendment" upon which to base the subsequent array of activism has an artificial or contrived quality. It is rather that the societal context that gave rise to the Settlement of 1937 continued to develop and to support a national perspective, which is discussed in the next chapter, and to express itself in the nationalization of civil liberties and civil rights standards that marked the Warren Court revolution. To say that the Constitution was "amended" in 1937 is to distort beyond usefulness the meaning of the word amend. The Constitution was not amended then, it was creatively developed, and the Settlement of 1937 and the Reconstruction are not the only times this has happened.

Despite the undemocratic aspects and potential of the process of creative constitutional development, some capacity for constitutional development is probably necessary for successful maintenance of constitutional democracy over the long term. There is no way of definitively proving or disproving this proposition. But an unsentimental look at history does arguably suggest it. The risks of permitting constitutional adjustment by other than the prescribed extraordinary majorities through formal processes are obvious, grave, and much discussed. But because extraordinary majorities are, by definition, extremely difficult to obtain, and because the risks to the nation of constitutional deadlock may sometimes be equally great, devices for constitutional leadership and development, and ultimately of legitimization, are probably necessary for survival of the system.

Of course, the fact that this historical tradition unquestionably exists does not in any way argue that it is good or wise or necessary or safe. Nor can it be proven that the British and American constitutional democratic systems would not have survived and ultimately evolved in more or less similar and progressive directions (or even developed in a much superior manner) over long periods of time without such mechanisms for constitutional development. Nor can it be maintained that every historical instance of "creative" constitutional development has been in some sense "legitimate" or for the best; clearly that is not so. But then, no one argues for democracy on the premise that majorities will always make correct decisions.

There are some grounds for suggesting that successful constitutional democracies (which both Britain and America qualify as, if longevity is a measure) need some kind of dynamic interaction between majoritarian and nonmajoritarian institutions, or at least structures, that can both defend and develop the prevailing constitutional understandings. These nonmajoritarian structures or institutions need not be courts and the processes involved in their functioning will indeed be messy and prone to error and abuse.

It seems unlikely that a philosophical formula, original historical intent, or an abstraction of fundamental values or of values inherent in the structure of government can provide much practical insight as to how and when the process of creative constitutional development should (will) or should not (will not) go forward. But hopefully, closer study of those instances when the process has gone forward will yield some further insight.

It is possible, of course, that we may only be able to say what is derivable from what is often supposed to have been said about democracy. Perhaps a democratic system with a nonmajoritarian mechanism that can sometimes alter the prevailing constitutional understandings is indeed prone to excessive imposition of elite values on the majority and other serious errors and is therefore, the worse possible kind of democratic system imaginable--except for a democratic system that does not have such a mechanism.

It is simply not possible to say that "We the People" occasionally "speak constitutionally" and that this somehow explains the important instances of successful constitutional development. People, institutions, and leaders are continuously speaking constitutionally and trying to develop the Constitution. Some efforts ultimately succeed and some fail and some succeed for a while and then fail. Some which succeed are accompanied by an electoral event and some are not, and some electoral events accompanied by constitutional issues result in constitutional development, while some do not.

The reasons for the success or failure of these efforts remain complex and multiple. Undoubtedly the fact that a very large number of people, if not a number able to mobilize a traditional constitutional majority, want what amounts to constitutional change is likely to be a major consideration in achieving and maintaining it. But popular demand is not the only consideration for sometimes change occurs even when the people may not much demand it. Clearly, some elements of the institutional leader-ship elite must want the change and their long run success likely will depend on the fit between what they try to impose and the actual or developing needs and interests of the emerging society.

Taken as a whole, much of what the Warren Court did reflected an attempt to address coherently the broad needs and trends of the emerging society. This is so even though many specific elements of particular decisions are arguably deficient. The contemporary effort at counterrevolution, which itself has been frequently marked by a self-conscious attempt at constitutional development, may succeed where it is confined to what can now be at least argued as doctrinal excesses that were the product of time-bound ideologies. Long-term success seems less likely where this effort attacks the underlying central thrust of its predecessor's efforts, which in turn reflected fundamental changes in the society of midcentury America--at least as long as those changes remain in place.

six/ The Changing Nature of American Pluralism

Despite the enormous debate and analysis asserting the inappropriateness and capriciousness of much of the judicial activism that is primarily associated with the Warren Court, most of such activism was both unavoidable and coherent. The activism was largely unavoidable because it was the product of the same social, economic, and political forces that produced the overall national centralization, and it was coherent because it expressed an integrated and principled perspective on what civil liberty should mean in the modern era. The extensive recent scholarly debate over the legitimacy of judicial activism has operated primarily on the philosophical level and has largely ignored the broad social, economic, and political context within which the activism in question actually occurred.

Civil liberties struggles, including those related to the Fourteenth Amendment, are conventionally depicted[1] as conflicts between the government and an individual. This is, of course, a valid mode of presentation, but it has tended to overshadow an equally valid one. The development of civil liberties, and civil liberties doctrine, has always been closely, perhaps primarily, connected with group conflicts.

In the Federalist Number 10, James Madison said that "Liberty is to faction what air is to fire." William Riker has stressed the close

---

1. For example, in Thomas Emerson, *Toward a General Theory of the First Amendment* (New York: Vintage Books, 1966), the first chapter entitled "The Function of Freedom of Expression in a Democratic Society" begins with: "The right of the individual to freedom of expression" Henry Abraham, *Freedom and the Court: Civil Rights and Liberties in the United States.* (New York: Oxford University Press, 1967) begins in the preface with: "This is essentially a study of the lines that must be drawn by a democratic society as it attempts to reconcile individual freedom with the rights of the community."

historical and functional relationship between "faction" and civil liberties, stating that "[r]esponsible popular government requires . . . the clarifying hand of faction" and that "a national atmosphere of the traditional democratic liberties is . . . the only condition in which faction will blaze up." Riker holds that in modern America, the ideals found in eighteenth-century bills of rights have become ends-in-themselves, seeing freedom of religion and expression, fair criminal procedures, and the like as having become an important part of the self-direction and self-respect we seek to obtain from democracy itself. As a result, he feels that people often forget that civil liberties have an institutional significance too; that "their original purpose was, in fact, not so much to dignify mankind as to foster faction and distribute dissent."[2]

It is widely understood that the historical origins of our major guarantees of civil liberty are rooted in factional conflict; that religious liberty was fashioned by and, in turn supports, the oldest sort of factionalism in Western Europe, and that most of the great Anglo-American procedural protections grew out of factional struggles between the English kings and their opponents.[3] But, perhaps because of our American philosophical tradition of individualism, when civil liberties are considered as a subject for current study, they are usually depicted by scholars as a part of this democratic ideal of "self-respect" and "self-direction."

Little recognition is normally given to the fact that civil liberties are "all of a method," that the "institutional significance" of civil liberties in democratic governments is not the elevation of the status of the individual, it is the encouragement of factions.[4] Thus civil liberties may well be defined as the institutional political arrangements that permit citizens who wish to defend, pursue, or promote varied cultural, economic, or political interests freely, openly, and peacefully to coalesce, organize, and interact toward their respective ends.

Accordingly, the development of civil liberties as both cause and effect of factional conflict is not limited historically to the English revolutionary period. The close relationship between civil liberties and factional conflict has continued down to the present day in our own country. Indeed the great nationalizing civil liberties revolution that

---

2. William Riker, *Democracy in the United States* (New York: Macmillan, 1963): 36, 91, 92.

3. See J. Legler, *Toleration and the Reformation*, 2 Vol. (New York: Association Press, 1960); John P. Roche, *Courts and Rights* (New York: Random House, 1966): 56-61.

4. Riker, *Democracy*, 91-92.

has been brought about by the Fourteenth Amendment over the last century has been intimately related to factional or group conflicts. Although frequently described as a process of making the guarantees of individual liberty contained in the Bill of Rights selectively binding upon the states, the development of the Fourteenth Amendment doctrine should also be described in terms of group or factional political conflicts and the changing pattern of American social and political pluralism.

The most notable example in the Warren Court era is the extensive development of free speech doctrine against the background of the civil rights conflict in the South. From *New York Times v. Sullivan*[5] to *Edwards v. South Carolina*,[6] the most significant group conflict of our time brought lasting change to First Amendment doctrine.

Nevertheless, such legal developments are still analyzed almost exclusively in terms of individuals and their rights. The Fourteenth Amendment is usually seen as a vehicle for imposing upon the states the great protections of individual liberties contained in the Bill of Rights, thus making the individual's freedom more secure by establishing national constitutional restraints applying to all levels of government.

Of course, most commentators would probably agree that the use of the equal protection clause to destroy the racial caste system in this country might be most aptly described as an extension of freedom not just for individuals but for an entire class of persons. Equal protection litigation has been traditionally concerned almost exclusively with claims of improper legislative classification, from the days of "separate but equal" to today's doctrine making race a suspect classification and holding all state racial classifications to a standard of strict scrutiny from which few emerge intact.

But few seem to recognize that almost all major Fourteenth Amendment decisions, including those decided on grounds of due process rather than equal protection, involve group or class rights and not just individual rights. One who did was Robert A. Horn, who as early as 1956 wrote "[t]oday a large volume of writing about civil liberties is . . . cast in terms of freedom of speech, press and assembly belonging to individuals. Yet the truth is that almost all these First Amendment and due process cases of this century deal with the rights of individuals acting as members of organized religious, political and economic associations."[7]

---

5. 376 U.S. 254 (1964).

6. 372 U.S. 299 (1963).

7. Robert A. Horn, *Groups and the Constitution* (New York: AMS Press, 1956), vii.

The picture of due process litigation that is usually put forward in most of the literature is one of the Supreme Court imposing or reiterating a general definition of civil liberty, and thus vindicating an individual plaintiff who had put forward a claim to some fundamental freedom that a state had failed to recognize. The fact is that most states do recognize virtually all of the major freedoms specified in the national Bill of Rights and have done so since well before the Court began the process of incorporation.[8] In the typical case, the Supreme Court is actually faced with a situation where the state action amounts to an explicit or implicit refusal to extend the guaranteed freedoms to one segment of its population.

Virtually all major instances of Supreme Court adjudication of the substantive aspects of prominent constitutional rights have not reflected a state acting to eliminate an entire freedom or to prohibit as criminal and anti-social the total exercise of some generally valued liberty. Rather, such cases have usually involved claims by or on behalf of a segment of the population to the effect that the established definition of the freedom in question was such as to improperly exclude them from its scope of protection.

The groups pressing substantive claims are often readily identifiable, particularly in First Amendment cases involving religion[9] or political free speech. Although procedural rights may be seen as more closely tied to peculiar individual circumstance, it remains apparent that the great expansion of procedural rights has been tied to an egalitarian effort to provide meaningful protection for racial minorities, the poor, and other disadvantaged groups.

In a polity with a significant amount of popular participation, laws that really do deny all or most of the population some important freedom will not normally be enacted. Thus, civil liberties questions usually arise when society stigmatizes as criminal, or at least fails to recognize as worthy or respectable, the valued activities or proclivities of a segment of the population. The Supreme Court is then called upon to "rescue" the segment.

---

8. F. N.Thorpe, *Federal and State Constitutions, Colonial Charters and Other Organic Laws of the States, Territories and Colonies Now or Heretofore forming the United States of America, Vols. I through VII*, (Washington, D.C.: Government Printing Office, 1909). B. P. Poore, *Federal and State Constitutions, Colonial Charters and Other Organic Laws of the U.S.* (Washington, D.C..: Government Printing Office, 1877); *Index Digest of State Constitutions* (Albany,N.Y.: New York State Constitutional Commission, 1915).

9. See for example, Wayne R. Swanson, *The Christ Child Goes to Court* (Philadelphia: Temple University Press, 1990).

True, litigation involving incorporated due process rights is usually pleaded on the formal ground that the incorporated Bill of Rights article in question requires the state to leave the individual plaintiff alone. But, in reality, the Court is usually being asked to extend the definition of a given freedom to cover the needs of a particular class of people and to determine that they should not be excluded from effective coverage because they constitute a legitimate, if peculiar social grouping (and are not merely representative individual examples of anti-social behavior capable of general and more or less random manifestation). This is not to say that the Court absolutely never develops or clarifies expansively doctrine regarding a basic right apart from the process of redefining it to extend it to a new group or to the new needs of an older group; clearly it sometimes does. But as a practical social, political, and historical matter, most of the pressure to stretch and redefine has in fact, and will likely continue to come from, such group conflict.

The distinction between those individuals whose behavior has been of a sort properly prohibited and those whose behavior should be permitted as incident to membership in a legitimate political or cultural grouping is, obviously, not always easily made. Nevertheless, the underlying issue in most major Fourteenth Amendment controversies is the the legitimacy of a claim of a segment of society to the equal exercise of basic liberties. Indeed, most due process civil liberties decisions of the Supreme Court could probably have been based upon the equal protection clause had the due process clause not existed, although, as a technical matter, the argument would perhaps have been more difficult to make.

While group analysis is not new to the political study of constitutional law, most efforts have been limited to pointing out the relation between the efforts of certain organized groups and the ultimate adjudication of specific cases in which they had an interest.[10] The argument here is that a kind of group analysis can be applied more

---

10. See for example, Clement Vose, "Litigation as a Form of Pressure Group Activity," *Annals of the American Academy of Political and Social Science* 319 (1958): 20; Vose, "The National Consumers League and the Brandeis Brief," *Midwest Journal of Political Science* 1 (1957): 276; Vose, *Caucasians Only: The Supreme Court, the N.A.A.C.P., and the Restrictive Covenant Cases* (Berkeley, University of California Press, 1959); J. Hackman, "Lobbying the Supreme Court: An Appraisal of Political Science Folklore," *Fordham Law Review* 35 (1966): 15; G. Caldeira and J. Wright, "Organized Interests and Agenda Setting in the U.S. Supreme Court," *American Political Science Review* (December 1988): 1109-1127.

broadly, that the overall evolution and development of Fourteenth Amendment doctrine that reached a peak of activity in the middle of the twentieth century--the process described as the nationalization of liberty--can be understood as reflecting and supporting the change in the overall pattern of relationships among politically and culturally significant groupings.

This changing pattern, in turn, reflects fundamental alterations in the social and economic context of American life. The development and reinterpretation of traditional concepts of American civil liberty to accommodate group relations in a national urban corporate society has been the principal constitutional business of the Supreme Court in recent decades. This has not been a linear process; it has been marked by doctrinal zigs and zags. Still, it is fair to say that the broad multidecade trend in twentieth-century America, which saw increasing centralization of governmental power in the national government, with the setting of regulatory standards in numerous areas of American economic and social life, had its counterpart in extensive and controversial Supreme Court activity.

To a considerable degree, that activism simply reflected both its context and a coherent and consistent perspective about the fair, neutral, and proper way to order liberty in America. The activism attempted to dismantle a different and older perspective, also fair and neutral by its lights. Both perspectives flow from the dynamics of the American political system and are legitimate within it.

The older perspective has its roots in agrarian America. It is decentralized and territorial. It sees freedom as the right of a group with shared values to acquire dominion over a territory and its government. National diversity, from this perspective, has been described as resembling a patchwork quilt. If an individual is not comfortable with the values being imposed through the government of a given area, he or she is theoretically free to move on to a patch on the quilt that is more comfortable. (Under certain circumstances, the individual may be able to gather together enough likeminded dissenters and keep moving until they are able to establish their own "patch.")[11] This perspective may be properly described as a federal perspective.

The newer perspective--a national perspective--is a product of urban, industrial, corporate America. It stresses the conditions that

11. John Roche, *The Quest for the Dream* (New York: Macmillan, 1963); John Roche, "American Liberty: An Examination of the Tradition of Freedom," "We've Never had more Freedom," in his *Shadow and Substance* (New York: Collier Books, 1964), 3, 39.

possible for people with the requisite skills to move and settle throughout much of the country without regard to their religious, racial, ethnic, political, or cultural backgrounds. It sees government as neutral, in that government is not to impose any group's particular values; indeed, it may even charge government with the obligation of affirmatively securing social neutrality in regard to these considerations.

To some extent, these divisions parallel the division between the "orthodox" and the "progressive" outlined by James Davison Hunter. He writes that "[i]t is out of the changing contours and shifting balance of pluralism that the key actors in the contemporary culture war emerge. . . . After the Second World War, the balance represented in the . . . consensus was . . . upset. Among the most important contributing factors has been the further expansion of pluralism."[12]

Many Americans remain attached to the federal perspective, and they doubtless see it as fair. They strongly resist the new developments and vigorously advance the federal perspective. The size and diversity of the nation permits many different varieties of group values to flourish, and the affirmation and support derived from local and state government structures is seen as essential to maintaining an effective sense of community. No interference is wanted from outside forces, especially the federal courts, and such interference is considered unfair. The agencies of federal interference are viewed as representatives of one narrow "secular" group tyrannizing over everyone else.

Those with attachment to what is here termed the national perspective view the federal perspective in reverse. They see each local community as an actual or potential tyranny, America as a whole as a vast aggregation of "vested heresies" restricting anyone who is different. They see the key role of the national government as preventing any group from using state or local government to establish a parochial set of values to oppress the different, the weak, or the helpless. According to the national perspective, government at all levels should be neutral, really neutral, in group value conflicts.

---

12. James Davison Hunter, *Culture Wars: The Struggle to Define America* (New York: Basic Books,1991): 67, 72. The federalist perspective also closely parallels what Michael Lind describes as the culture of Anglo-Saxon America in *The Next American Nation* (New York: Free Press, 1995). The emergence of the national perspective would parallel the emergence of what he terms Euro-America. What he terms Multicultural America would describe the period of cultural conflict of the last two decades, the long-term impact of which remains ambiguous.

In this context, the midcentury conception of judicial restraint, with its tenets that the Supreme Court and the lower federal courts should move cautiously to alter society, should express a deference to the "political" branches of government, and should show a respect for the diversity of the federal system, too often becames a defense of the injustices that have been historically associated with the federal perspective. Most midcentury judicial activism, which the federal perspective sees as busybody social engineering and the attempt to destroy traditional, "real" values through a questionable and highly ideological hypersensitivity to dubious social claims, is seen quite differently from the national perspective. The national government, through the agency of the Supreme Court and the federal courts, is nationalizing liberty. It is achieving the true neutrality that should have been by breaking up unfair attempts by parochial groups to establish their own values through the seizure of political power and the use of it to retard the interests and rights of perceived social and philosophical adversaries.

Robert Post describes federalism as "a form of cultural pluralism that valorizes the diversity of local cultures. . . . By focusing on the individual as the privileged unit of legal and social analysis, the incorporation decisions eliminated local cultural variations. . . . These decisions . . . crushed federalism as an effective counter to the logic of individual liberty."[13]

It is an exaggeration to see federalism as "crushed," and individuals, in fact, do continue to maintain subcultural and other group affiliations. What is "eliminated" are the advantages that specific "local cultural variations" have had maintained by state and local governmental authority; the variations themselves are free to continue. others are better able to flourish as well. Obviously unique and purely individual perspectives and styles are also freer to develop, as Post suggests. Nevertheless, to reiterate Robert Horn's point cited earlier, "[t]he truth is that almost all these First Amendment and due process cases of this century deal with the rights of individuals acting as members of organized religious, political and economic associations."[14]

Seen from the national perspective, the product of midcentury activism is simple fairness, and the complaints about such activism are not the shouts of injured democrats who are loath to see their cherished political process short-circuited. They are the squeals of wounded

---

13. Robert C. Post, "William J. Brennan and the Warren Court" in *The Warren Court in Historical and Political Perspective,* Mark Tushnet, ed. (Charlottesville: University Press of Virginia, 1993), 126-127.

14. Horn, *Groups and the Constitution,* vii.

privilege, the cries of groups whose dominant social interests or values are threatened by opening up America to real neutrality and the changes that become possible thereby.

Of course, the nature of the national perspective has become complicated in recent years because some that have been associated with it are clearly advocates of using government, usually the national government, to act explicitly and affirmatively on behalf of groups who, often plausibly, see themselves as having been seriously disadvantaged by traditional arrangements and are thus, "due" remedial measures. This tendency has raised some difficult unresolved questions about the national perspective's association with government neutrality.

The multidecade process through which the national perspective emerged as the Supreme Court nationalized the minimum standards for civil liberty in America, when taken as a whole rather than through any one of its particulars, reflected fundamental social and economic changes in the society. The claim is not that the process was absolutely inevitable in some historical determinist sense. But changes in the society eroded the older pattern of pluralism, and when the newer pattern did emerge, the process was appropriate to these changes in the context. The process of emergence persisted beyond the time of the Warren Court, which gave rise to most of it and with which it is most closely identified, because the process through which the national perspective emerged drew support from and simultaneously gave support to this context.

Judicial activism on behalf of the national perspective has had a vehicle with which it has come to be particularly identified--the Fourteenth Amendment to the Constitution. It is probably not an exaggeration to say that the Fourteenth Amendment embodies the national perspective on civil liberty. Put aside the technical legal gloss that has grown around the amendment and look instead at the debates that led to its enactment-not as has become fashionable, for the purpose of finding the answer to some specific legal question, but to get an idea of the atmosphere and sensibility of the Congress that enacted it. Do so and you will find all over the pages of the *Congressional Globe* the national perspective: modern, high-minded, and cosmopolitan.[15]

The reaction of the late nineteenth century almost buried this spirit and turned the Fourteenth Amendment for a time into a vehicle for the

---

15. The national perspective is most apparent in the debates of the Reconstruction Congress; see in particular the *Congressional Globe* of the Thirty-Ninth Congress, 1st Session (1865) and that of the Forty-Second Congress, 1st Session, Appendix (1872).

protection of corporate industrial development from government economic regulation. (It is worthy of note, though, that the two principal purposes for which the amendment has been used in its thirteen decades are both the product of the same underlying economic and social trends. The national perspective on civil liberty, which found in the amendment its vehicle for implementation, derives its ultimate rationale from urban, corporate industrialism, which the court overprotected from state regulation in the gone-but-not-forgotten era of substantive due process.)

The national perspective was revived in this century, particularly at midcentury, and the handful of words in the Fourteenth Amendment's first section have had a truly seminal impact upon our constitutional law. These few Fourteenth Amendment phrases (along with the interstate commerce clause) are the most important phrases in modern American constitutional law. They are the foundation upon which the nationalization of liberty has been constructed.

Of course, what are arguably the most sweeping words in the amendment have had little impact. In the *Slaughter-House Cases*[16] by a 5-4 vote, the Supreme Court refused to concede that the privileges or immunities of United States citizens (referred to in the first clause of section one after the phrase defining United States citizenship) included anything more than those rights inherent in the very existence of the national government. This was done despite the fact that such an interpretation made the clause meaningless since the power to order the states to refrain from interfering with those privileges and immunities inherent in the very existence of the national government was recognized even before the passage of the Fourteenth Amendment.

Justice Bradley's dissenting opinion points out that before the Fourteenth Amendment, state citizenship was held to be primary in America, and the securing of the basic rights of free men, which Americans were understood to have derived from their English legal heritage, was thus in the hands of the states. However, Bradley argues, since the Fourteenth Amendment now makes national citizenship primary, the national government may surely now prevent the states from violating the broad category of basic rights. He expresses his belief that the privileges or immunities of United States citizens referred to in the Fourteenth Amendment were intended to include all the fundamental rights of citizens, not just the narrow category cited by the majority.

---

16. 83 U.S. (16 Wall.) 36 (1873).

It is true the general objective sought by the petitioners in the *Slaughter-House Cases,* that of obtaining recognition of a federal judicial power to set aside legislation that violates basic rights, was ultimately accomplished by means of the due process clause. But there is one important difference. The due process theory does not claim that the rights protected are federal rights. It recognizes that the responsibility for securing them remains in the hands of the states, but it holds that the requirements of due process prevent the states themselves from violating them. Plenary federal authority over private action interfering with these rights is thus not conferred.

From the beginning of its use as the primary vehicle for both the nationalization of liberty and the vindication of the national perspective, continuing down to the present day, the due process clause of the Fourteenth Amendment has encountered some notable difficulties with its operating theoretical framework. This was perhaps most dramatically illustrated in *Griswold v. Connecticut.*[17] In that case a majority struck down Connecticut's law prohibiting use of contraceptives by announcing that law's conflict with a constitutional right of privacy. But the justices could not agree on the source of this right. Some thought it was to be found in penumbras around the First, Fourth, and Fifth Amendments; some thought it was incorporated as one of the unnamed Ninth Amendment rights; and others thought that the right could not be found in the Bill of Rights at all, but that it was a part of the concept of ordered liberty inherent in the due process clause itself.

But this considerable disagreement over a seemingly vital matter in doctrinal development has not had any practical consequences. The right of privacy has been established even though the justices could not agree on its source, and the right was later extended to cover abortions in *Roe v. Wade.*[18]

The equal protection clause, the other great vehicle for activism, has had its own problems. Yet these difficulties too have not halted the development of doctrine. Perhaps that is because the effort to establish the national perspective through the amendment in the middle decades of this century really rested upon the sense that the amendment embodies it, rather than on one or another technical theory of how the amendment operates. As doctrine that reflects the perspective evolved under the rubric of the amendment, the belief became a reality.

---

17. 381 U.S. 479 (1965).
18. 410 U.S. 113 (1973).

The century during which much of the change in the pattern of group relationships and the major development of Fourteenth Amendment civil liberties doctrine occurred has been also a period of major social change in America. It has, of course, been a time of urbanization and industrialization with the decline of the old, rural small-town America and the rise of a modern, cosmopolitan, urban and suburban nation. The earlier America has been described as largely founded by people escaping from oppressive environments who found the new land marked by rather free geographic mobility. "As a result, most colonials who dissented from their own community's conception of right and justice could move without great difficulty to a more congenial community."[19]

John Roche observes that America's early years were not the "golden age" of freedom that some like to believe. He claims that whatever diversity of opinion existed "was a consequence not of tolerance and mutual respect . . . but of the existence of many communities within the society, each with its own canons of orthodoxy." To put it another way, if an individual searched long and hard, he or she could probably find somewhere in America a community that shared his or her own particular political, cultural, religious, or other views and, once that person joined that community, he or she could help impose its group beliefs on others: "a microcosm to be intolerant with." This picture of the older America recognizes that "while there was no centralized authoritarian state on the European model . . . the centralized state is not the only institution capable of oppression; the parish can be as severe in its impact on the individual as the centralized variety" and further, that "the U.S. was notoriously the happy hunting ground of what Reisman has acutely termed 'vested heresies.'"[20]

According to this view, the United States in its early period was not really an integrated national community but a "number of subcultures living side by side within the geographic expanse of the

---

19. Ely, *Democracy and Distrust*, 178, citing Louis Hartz, *The Liberal Tradition in America* (New York: Harcourt Brace, 1955), 64-65 and quoting Nelson, "The Eighteenth-Century Background of John Marshall's Constitutional Jurisprudence,"*Michigan Law Review 76 (1978)*: 893, 921. See also, e.g. Madison's "Memorial and Remonstrance against Religious Assessments" Section 10, quoted in *Everson v. Board of Education*, 330 U.S. 1, 69 (1947) (appendix to opinion of Rutledge, J. dissenting).

20. Roche, *The Quest for the Dream*; Roche, "We've Never had more Freedom," 39; "American Liberty,"3, 8-9.

nation."[21] Andrew Hacker has commented that "the majority of Americans spent their lives in circumscribed settings which, if not literally feudal, nevertheless forced regimens that tolerated little deviation from established local standards."[22]

David Hackett Fischer has described at length what he believes to have been the four dominant regional cultures that populated America beginning around 1629.[23] He argues that these cultures and their folkways dominated particular areas of the new land and were derived from particular regions of England. The dominant four are the Puritan in Massachusetts, the Cavalier in Virginia, the Quaker in the Delaware Valley, and the backcountry people sometimes called the Scots-Irish who settled the southern highlands of Appalachia.

He also mentions several additional cultures that dominated other specific geographic areas, the largest being New Netherland, which occupied much of the Hudson Valley. Another developed along the coast of South Carolina, comprised of families from the West Indies, French Huguenots, and some emigrants from tidewater Virginia, with slaves that came from the Congo basin and Angola. These groups are described as developing a unique culture closer to the Caribbean colonies than to the Chesapeake. Yet another was in North Carolina's Cape Fear Valley, settled by the Highland Scots in about 1732.

Freedom in the early republic was essentially conceived of in corporate terms, and the institutions created at the founding of our nation were not intended to threaten this arrangement. They were meant to secure the local communities from the threat of central tyranny but were not concerned with the tyranny that often existed within each subcultural unit.

Roche has argued that this pattern broke down in twentieth century America, and he attributed its demise to urbanization, industrialization, and the rise of elites concerned with civil liberties that have "infiltrated" the ever more powerful national government. The effect has been to produce a new pattern: a society marked by impersonality and the "bureaucratization" of interpersonal and intergroup conflict.

The two patterns outlined here are, of course, reflected in some manner in much of classic social theory, though no one describes them exactly. These kinds of theories, which describe modern industrializing

---

21. David Hackett Fischer, *Albion's Seed: Four British Folkways in America* (New York: Oxford University Press, 1989): 783.

22. Andrew Hacker, *The End of the American Era* (New York: Atherton, 1970), 209.

23. Fischer, *Albion's Seed*, 783-819.

societies as moving from "status to contract" (Henry Maine), or from "Gemeinschaft to Gesellschaft" (Ferdinand Tonnies), or from "community to association" (Robert MacIver), suggest that at some level, some of what has been described here in America reflects the broader consequences of modernization and industrialization. The point is not that the movement from a sort of American Gemeinschaft to Gesellschaft made historically inevitable each and every Warren Court decision that has been criticized as activist. It is rather that the agenda of modern post-1930s activism as set forth reasonably accurately in the preferred position footnote,[24] with its stress on the rights of insular and discrete minorities, was not some sort of eccentric whim of a transient majority of justices. This agenda reflected some very broad long-term underlying societal trends.

In sum, the older pattern is one in which Americans are grouped into geographic subcultures of shared attitudes and intolerant dispositions possessing direct majority control of the local legal and political apparatus, thus assuring institutional support or acquiescence for their point of view.[25] This situation is most viable only when the degree of

---

24. *U.S. v. Carolene Products*, 304 U.S. 144, 152-153 n.4 (1938). As discussed earlier, this famous footnote, written at the time the Court was enshrining the post-Court-packing crisis Settlement of 1937 and deferring to legislatures in matters of social and economic policy, suggested that certain rights specifically protected by the Constitution and its amendments might have a preferred position and deserve special judicial protection.

25. A vigorous defense of the older pattern can be found in Wendell Berry's *Sex, Economy. Freedom and Community* (New York: Pantheon, 1993). Here Berry attributes sexual and economic brutality to the turning away from traditional forms of community. He says that "[t]here is in fact a good deal of talk about pluralism these days but most of it that I have seen is fashionable, superficial, and virtually worthless. It does not foresee or advocate a plurality of settled communities but is only a sort of indifferent charity toward a plurality of aggrieved groups and individuals."

"The social and cultural pluralism that some now see as a goal is a public of destroyed communities. Wherever it exists, it is the result of centuries of imperialism. The modern industrial urban centers are `pluralistic' because they are full of refugees from destroyed communities . . . The pluralists who see this state of affairs as some sort of improvement or as the beginning of `global culture' are being historically perverse. They wish to regard liberally and tolerantly the diverse, sometimes competing claims and complaints of a rootless society, and yet they continue to tolerate also the ideals and goals of the industrialism that caused the uprooting. They affirm the pluralism of a society formed by the uprooting of cultures at the same time that they regard the fierce self-defense of still-rooted cultures as 'fundamentalism' for which

economic and political interdependence required on a national basis is minimal. Such was the case in an America with a rural economy shielded from serious problems of national defense by two large oceans and weak neighbors.

The economic requirements of modern industrial America stress interdependence. People with skills are required; they must move to places where their skills are needed; large numbers of people must live, work, and educate themselves in densely populated urban areas. Modern transportation and communication produce constant subcultural interpenetration. It thus becomes increasingly difficult for a subculture to encompass all its members in a limited geographic area. Persons affiliated with one or another of these subcultures are increasingly required to spend a large amount of their time together with members of other subcultures in activities to which the subcultural affiliation is essentially irrelevant.

But the subcultures do not all disappear; many persist and many new ones form.[26] While people today may cluster together in small neighborhood area "lifestyle" groups, these areas are typically much smaller than in previous centuries and much less self-contained. They usually do not combine either economic activity or significant political control.[27] The people will normally work elsewhere, outside their

---

they have no tolerance at all . . . And when these cultures again attempt self-defense--when they again assert the inseparability of culture and place--they are opposed by this pluralistic society as self-righteously as ever."

"A culture capable of preserving land and people can be made only within a relatively stable and enduring relationship between a local people and its place . . . There can . . . be no national policy of pluralism and multiculturalism but only these pluralities of local cultures" (pp. 169-171).

26. Despite the diversity of modern America, there remains a somewhat surprising religious dominance of particular geographic areas: Baptists in the South (though they are not significant elsewhere); Lutherans in the upper Midwest farmbelt; Roman Catholics in the Northeast; and Mormons in Utah and the Rocky Mountain states. See Barry A. Kosmin and Seymour P. Lachman, *One Nation Under God: Religion in Contemporary Society* (New York: Harmany Books, 1993), 51-113.

27. Some insight into how elements of the old pattern persist within the newer pattern can be derived from Michael J. Weiss, *The Clustering of America* (New York: Harper and Row,1988). The book is based upon the PRIZM system, a computerized system that sorts the nation's 36,000 ZIP codes into 450 lifestyle clusters for target marketing. Used primarily for commercial purposes, and also for political marketing, it is a mix of old ethnic characteristics with economic and other factors. According to the book,

neighborhoods, and usually in organizations to which their "lifestyle" groupings are essentially irrelevant. They will demand a political and legal system that fully tolerates, and indeed, validates the legitimacy of their differences, and they will resist its falling into the hands of forces that would deny them this legitimacy.

Today's America is a very different kind of patchwork quilt, much more intricate than the old one. It has been described by Weiss as a nation where "neighborhoods separated geographically can be virtually identical in lifestyle"; "[o]n a cluster map, people who live 3000 miles apart yet share the same neighborhood type have more in common with each other than with those people who live only three miles away." People who "belong" to a lifestyle cluster that is geographically dispersed into pockets all around the country are subject to the same social and lifestyle trends, and will respond to the same messages, commercial and political, in similar ways. And reciprocally, people within such a geographically dispersed lifestyle cluster will likely have many similar expectations.[28]

Such developments that have so changed America were arguably necessary for the maintenance of political stability. Robert Dahl's writings suggest that in nations where people live their whole lives within a territorial subcultural unit, the potential for explosive conflict between such units is likely to be high.[29] Yet to describe, as Dahl does, what has happened in the United States as ethnic and subcultural "assimilation" is something of an oversimplification.

In the gradual development of church-state separation in the Western world, which helped maintain civil peace in nations with significant religious divisions within the population, there is a sense in which the growth of religious toleration, arising from the separation of the religious from the political realm, does reflect or enforce a kind of redefinition of religion. Certainly this seems so at least insofar as religion's encompassing of the political realm was previously seen as essential to its nature.

But it would be inaccurate to describe such separation in terms that imply the end of significant religious difference. By the same token, the new pattern of pluralism, which not only enforces separation of the political and religious realms at the local governmental level, but does so in large measure as a result of the separation of religious, ethnic, and

---

pockets of a particular cluster can be often found in localities all around the country.

28. Weiss, *Clustering*, 6.

29. Robert A. Dahl, *Democracy and Its Critics* (New Haven, Conn.: Yale University Press, 1989), 254-260.

other subcultures from the economic realm as well, may be seen by some as radically diminishing the impact and importance of subcultural affiliation.

Again, this is certainly the case to the extent that encompassing the economic realm is viewed as intrinsic to the nature of the subculture, but it is inaccurate to describe this process as the end of all significant subcultural difference. These differences do not have as great an impact on the lives of their members as they would be if they dominated the political and economic aspects of those lives, but the subcultural differences remain significant within many aspects of life.

Some traditional ethnic or religious differences may not survive or at least, may not be as influential among large numbers of people if they do not also dominate the political and economic aspects of life. To the extent their influence is diminished over many people, one could describe those people as "assimilated." Yet since those people will form into new and differing subcultural, political, and economic groupings, and in many instances may do so in ways that show connections to the older affiliations, assimilation really may not be a fully descriptive term.

Peter Drucker says that "both society and polity in developed countries are now full of power centers that are outside of, and separate from, government. The new pluralism in society focuses on function and performance. It is a pluralism of single-purpose organizations, each concerned with one social task: wealth creation or schooling or health care or forming the values and habits of the young."[30] He sees these developments as part of a long-term trend where social tasks that 150 years ago were done, if at all, within the family, are now done in and through organized single-purpose institutions. He notes that the pluralism of today's institutions is different from that of the past in that it is based on function rather than power.

It might be more accurate to say that they have legitimate power only within their functional area. Thus people belonging to different subcultural groups work together in the institutions based upon skills they have that are suitable for the function because skill, and not subcultural affiliation, is the relevant consideration. On the other hand, the power of the social and economic institutions Drucker describes is normally not available to support any particular subcultural group.

---

30. Peter F. Drucker, *The New Realities* (New York: Harper and Row, 1989), 76, and Chapter 7 generally.

Alan Wolfe argues that Americans have chosen to be modern, not ethnic; that America has solved the problem of ethnicity that plagues other nations by transcending it. He says that groups do not live in peace with each other in the United States, individuals do. While this is substantially true, it is also true that some elements of traditional ethnicity remain quite powerful in America, both in their hold over individuals and as determinants of social behavior, and many modern subcultural groupings have elements of traditional ethnicity within them. It is hard not to agree with Wolfe that the more traditional and classic ethnic arrangements "have a way of encouraging their people, when not killing each other over roots, to retreat into that special kind of narrowness and superstition that ethnicity alone can legitimate." And there is a sense in which modern cultural arrangements can be fairly described as "low cost."[31]

But to say that subcultural groupings no longer dominate or order the political and economic realms of life, and that the individual's freedom of action is thereby maximized, is not to say that these groupings may not affect the political or economic behavior of their members. The evidence is that they definitely do impact such behavior in many instances.[32]

Although what Roche terms the "bureaucratization of civil liberties" tends to reinforce the perspective of a series of individuals claiming arbitrary or discriminatory treatment, on the whole the major attacks upon and victories for civil liberties remain, at root, the product of group conflicts. The frequent inability of many groups to obtain satisfactory results from state and local governments, which retain the relevant police powers and often use them to reinforce the older pattern of pluralism, has led them to seek national intervention to secure their equal rights.[33] Operating, in a sense, as the agent of the evolving newer

---

31 See Alan Wolfe,"The Return of the Melting Pot," *The New Republic*, 31 December 1990: 27, 30 (a review of four books on ethnicity).

32. See among other works, Kevin Phillips, *The Emerging Republican Majority* (New Rochelle, N.Y.:Arlington House, 1969). See also Garry Wills, *Under God: Religion and American Politics* (New York: Simon and Schuster, 1990).

33. A professor at a prominent New England College, though not overly taken himself by much of the Warren Court's work product, nevertheless reports a conversation with a Federal Circuit Court judge that supports this point. The judge seemed to feel that, theories aside, the professor did not appreciate the pressures on judges from people who move in from other parts of the country and take to the courts when they find that various rights they "expected" were not being effectively or sufficiently recognized.

pattern, the Supreme Court frequently, if imperfectly, used the Fourteenth Amendment as a vehicle to extend basic liberties to these political, racial and cultural minorities during the middle and later decades of the twentieth century.

seven/ The Durability of the Warren Court Legacy

This book has attempted to contribute to the understanding of the judicial activism associated with the Warren Court by arguing that consideration of the broader context within which it occured sheds light on the persistence of its most important accomplishments. The effort developed out a sense that much of the contemporary academic context, which is focused upon normative considerations, is circular and cannot ultimately resolve the issues it raises satisfactorily on its own terms.

The book looked to the political context and the light that is cast when judicial activism is considered as a part of a broad contemporary bureaucratic and institutional context. It then pointed to the historical context and argued that creative constitutional development has always characterized the Anglo-American tradition. Finally, it considered Warren Court activism in its social context, as operating to adjust doctrine to the changing pattern of American pluralism. The contention here is that the Court's "nationalization of civil liberties" succeeded and has largely persisted because of its "fit" with the "needs" of that pattern.

De Tocqueville observed that most major conflicts in America ultimately become lawsuits. This is sometimes cited as a sort of given of our culture that supports, among other things, the acceptance of judicial review. But if we assume that a mechanism performing the constitutional development function is necessary to the success and longevity of our political system and that other devices, structures, or classes may perform the function elsewhere, something more may then be learned from his parallel observation that lawyers are a kind of aristocracy in America. America has no real aristocracy or establishment to develop the Constitution. It began with a weak sense of national community, and Hamilton's efforts to create a national federalist establishment fell apart--except in a sense, in the Court where the Federalist agenda found something of a home.

Historically, most broad instances of successful judicial activism over time seem to have been primarily concerned with promoting aspects of nation-building, reflecting the values and agendas of significant portions of the continually changing and developing national elite. Much of the early activism was concerned with early development of national commerce, the interest of the incipient national market, and with the powers of Congress and the Court to promote and protect it. Interestingly, the Court's effort in the *Dred Scot* case to "save" the union by rejecting any effective concept of national citizenship did not work.

The effort to protect a national free market by rejecting state regulatory power and then national regulatory power worked for a while but itself met rejection with the growing perception that it was necessary to restrict somewhat the freedom of large-scale corporate enterprise and to build a limited national welfare state. The jury is still out on the Court's largely passive acceptance of much of the national defense state.

The major work of the Court in recent decades has focused on impacting local power structures and establishing national standards for civil liberties and civil rights throughout the nation. The Constitution was not amended; the vehicle in the form of the Fourteenth Amendment was already in place, but it has been much developed. Although the Court has been much criticized for its efforts and has provoked enormous debate over the legitimacy of much of its activity, as discussed, it is remarkable how, despite this debate and the opposition to specific decisions, so much doctrinal change that developed during this period has been absorbed into law and broad consensus.

That is not simply because conservatives are trapped by the conservative obligation to hold to stare decisis; recent years have shown that some are prepared to ignore it when it suits them. Rather it is because, when looked at from the broad perspective of the social-economic context, we can see that most of what was done was hardly an arbitrary exercise. It was not primarily driven by philosophical or ideological beliefs though these were often present and visible in the emerging constitutional doctrine. Instead, the Warren Court revolution was driven by new societal relationships and thus, in a sense, by the evolving needs of midcentury American society.

Some readers will quarrel with this argument on the grounds that it suggests but ignores a number of questions they find disturbing. Is it right for justices to engage in creative constitutional development even if it is true that it has sometimes worked out by providing a "useful" or "necessary" adjustment? Does not the argument, therefore, suggest that justices should attempt to perceive underlying long term societal trends and "needs" and, if they feel they have done so and that they can act in harmony with what they have perceived, should they then feel free to aggressively "go to it"? Is this not an invitation to the worst kinds of abuse?

Providing answers to those questions is not the purpose of this book. Nor is the suggestion offered earlier that the recent stress on normative theory may have reached diminishing returns an argument that normative considerations should be ignored altogether or forever. It is rather a claim that it might be more fruitful for now to concentrate on understanding the broader significance of what actually seems to have occurred.

It is because most major doctrinal innovations of midcentury Supreme Court activism were animated by the evolving national perspective and reflected underlying changes in the basic overall pattern of relationships among politically and culturally significant groupings that so much of the most important doctrine has persisted, despite deliberate conservative efforts to change the makeup of the Court's personnel since the late 1960s. Midcentury activism may now be seen as a part of the overall nationalization of political authority in Washington in the first three quarters of this century.

The long-run impact of the New Deal on the Court was to demolish the older conservative judicial activism in the economic area that stood as an obstacle to the completion of the New Deal's legislative program and to prepare the groundwork for its replacement by a newer activism, which set national standards in the area of civil liberties behavior. In this sense, the Court's activity since the 1930s paralleled the New Deal's centralization of economic authority in the legislative and executive branches. As the administrations and Congresses of the 1960s completed much of the New Deal's unfinished legislative agenda, the Warren Court largely completed the judicial nationalization of civil liberties and civil rights by bringing selective incorporation of the Bill of Rights through the Fourteenth Amendment to the point of virtual totality, and through vigorous reinterpretation of the equal protection clause.

Whatever criticism some may have today of specific aspects of this nationalizing process, we can see that these decades brought to substantial fruition a great historic centralizing movement aimed at securing for excluded groups the right to participate in the larger American society--its national, corporate integrated economy, and its substantially democratic polity. Of course, this movement has always been primarily a public movement tied to an expansion of the public sector, a broader conception of public obligation and entitlement, and constitutionally, to an expanded notion of state action. The movement managed to serve at once the American democratic tradition as it is usually understood, the perceived interests of millions of American citizens, and the functional needs of the society's major economic institutions and activities.

The universal values associated with this nationalizing process have been and remain vital to the major institutions of the American economy, and it is doubtful that we will find the American constitutional system operating in a manner that frustrates this need. But it is unclear as we approach the twenty-first century whether the needs of the national, and now international, postindustrial economy will serve to support continued application of these values within a broad, vigorous public sector. In other words, it is possible, though hardly certain, that the confluence of the American democratic tradition, the functional needs of large and significant economic institutions, and the interests of millions of Americans that produced the political and constitutional expansion of a centralized public sector in the middle of the twentieth century, may now be pulling apart.

The two-decade effort to mount a counterrevolution on the Supreme Court has altered some aspects of specific Warren Court doctrines, and some of these changes seem likely to persist. But thus far, much of the core doctrinal developments of Warren Court activism have survived because they have fit the broader context--the needs of the larger developing society. The larger question now is will the continuing attack by some members of today's Court on the underlying central thrust of its predecessor's efforts ultimately succeed because the context that supported that thrust is changing?

Certainly there are much noted trends toward privatization of information, communication, and education in contemporary America.[1] America's public schools have been the principal arena of modern constitutional controversy because they significantly influence what values and perspectives are transmitted to the next generation, leading to battles for control of the transmission process over issues like prayer,

1. For a description of "overclass" behavior leading to isolation and insulation from the broader society, see Lind, *The Next American Nation*.

busing, affirmative action, and censorship. But if the upper middle class abandons the public schools, opposes the taxes required to properly support them, and sends its own declining numbers of children to private schools, with or without vouchers or tuition tax credits, the significance of public schools in our society will be much reduced.

The concept of the public forum was expanded and protected by the Warren Court in the civil rights demonstration cases and other decisions. But in the early 1970s, the Burger Court undermined early trends toward expanding the public forum into privately owned suburban shopping centers.[2] As suburbanization continues, with privately owned areas not subject to the Constitution increasingly serving as the centers of community commerce and gathering, the impact of public forums in our affairs becomes diminished.

The 1950s and 1960s saw enormous growth in the influence of television and a growing dominance of television by the then three major national networks. What they did, for good or bad, tended to determine the national conversation and gave it a strong element of unity. In this limited competitive environment, some effort was occasionally put forth toward obtaining the status rewards that accrued for offering the most comprehensive and serious news department. The result of cable and related developments has been vast choice for television viewers, but the much accelerated competition for viewers has impacted the national conversation and many feel, significantly degraded it. Certainly the availability of numerous viewing options has contributed to a significant fragmentation of the national audience.

The breakup of the regulated telephone monopoly, the growth of cable television (which has been subjected alternately to either little or no regulation), and the increased and increasingly revolutionary role of personal computers and the "information highway" in the lives of most Americans are all producing significant societal change. What has already occurred in the communications revolution, according to most observers, is minimal compared to what is projected for the next two decades.

But if the public schools are abandoned by the privileged, if traditional public forums decline, and if people make their personal information selections from an increasingly vast array of limited-access sources, what remains of public education and communication in the

---

2. *Amalgamated Food Employees v. Logan Valley Plaza*, 391 U.S. 308 (1968); *Lloyd v. Tanner*, 407 U.S. 551 (1972); *Hudgens v. N.L.R.B.*, 424 U.S. 507 (1976).

traditional sense might then be left to languish in the hands of those less committed to the national perspective. More important, the cumulative impact of these societal trends could be to drastically reduce the practical social and political impact of public forums, publicly regulated (and "free") information media, and public educational institutions, as all of these are traditionally understood.

Thus, even without shrinking the scope of constitutional rights attached to these things, the Court, by essentially doing nothing to reinterpret the concepts to make them meaningful to the changing society, can diminish them almost as effectively as if it set out to methodically reverse them. It is this fate, rather than outright reversal, that may well await significant portions of the Warren Court's revolution. This could conceivably happen even if new appointees move the Court more toward the ideological center.

But such developments are certainly not inevitable and indeed, it is most likely that even if these tendencies continue to play themselves out for a period, the ultimate fate of the Warren Court's doctrinal innovations will not be complete irrelevance. Ironically, if the efforts of recent decades to reformulate doctrine in ways that would lead to greater social integration and the stabilization of intergroup relationships in America had been more successful, and if the nature of the groups involved had itself been stable, then the trend toward privatization might prove more workable over the long run.

Of course, if these efforts had been more successful, the trend toward privatization might not have occurred in the first place. That trend, with its accompanying hostility to government bureaucracy and particularly to the federal government, has many causes, but certainly hostility to the public sector is in no small part hostility to groups that are perceived as the primary beneficiaries of public sector interest and concern.

The nature of the groups that make up America is not stable. They are changing dramatically. America is now experiencing demographic changes[3] that are creating a more radically diverse country than has ever been imagined possible, and this is occurring in an increasingly international world economy.

If immigration and birthrate trends continue, at some point in the next century the majority of the country's population will be non-White. Religious traditions that cannot be encompassed within the Judeo-Christian rubric will be significantly represented within the

---

3. Alejandro Portes and Ruben G. Rumbaut, *Immigrant America: A Portrait* (Berkeley: University of California Press, 1990).

population. The role of women in the important work institutions of the nation seems likely to continue to develop, with women achieving ever increasing prominence. There will be other changes too in the makeup of the society that will raise profound and inescapable challenges to established concepts of civil liberties and civil rights.

It seems inevitable that these radical changes will force a return to systematic consideration of issues raised by this still-changing pluralism. The problem is that these issues really cannot be effectively and systematically considered as public issues if they manifest themselves in increasingly privatized circumstances.

Another way of looking at the problem is that the challenge (or threat) that such extreme diversity unaccommodated will pose to the very survival of fundamental American ideas may be such as to require a new definition and expansion of the notion of "publicness." If there is not in some meaningful sense an important public sector in which political and legal relationships among these groups can be worked out, within which traditional constitutional doctrine can be reformulated and made meaningful to the new society and the minimum necessary amount of social integration thus achieved and maintained, then by definition the society and the values enshrined in traditional doctrine cannot effectively survive.

Of course, the nature of this newly expanded public sector is not knowable. It probably will involve some new notions of what is public and these may not be easily envisioned today. The question of what is public and what is not has always been one of the central and unresolved questions contained within the Fourteenth Amendment. The *Civil Rights Cases*[4] have never been explicitly reversed because Congress finally acted in the mid-1960s under the interstate commerce power that the Court had so dramatically expanded three decades earlier. It is not to be doubted, however, that if Congress had not acted, the Warren Court would have. It likely would have gone so far as to find that all privately owned places of public accommodation are sufficiently infused with state action as to be subject to the coverage of the amendment. It might have extended *Shelley v. Kraemer*[5] to hold

---

4. 109 U.S. 3 (1883).

5. *Shelley v. Kraemer*, 334 U.S. 1 (1948). This controversial case held that use of the Courts to enforce racially restrictive covenants in deeds constituted impermissible state action in violation of the Fourteenth Amendment. In other words, private parties can constitutionally insert such provisions in deeds, but their enforcement in the Court is unconstitutional.

The case's rationale has been criticized by some as undermining private property rights. Does the case mean that if a landowner posts his land but

that use of public police and judicial processes to enforce discriminatory relationships in such businesses violates the amendment. Similar and other creative doctrine likely would have extended the obligations of equal protection to corporate business.

There are clues that suggest these likely results that can be derived from a close reading of the decisions of the Court of the early 1960s; this is not simply speculation. But any effort to delineate now the nature of the public sector that some Court of the future may shape is not possible.

Just as economic and technological changes have encouraged privatization in recent years, other such changes will shape the process of redefinition of the public sector by any Court (or Congress) that undertakes the job of meeting the challenge presented by the new American pluralism. Similarly, while we can project some sense of what the new American pluralism will look like as well as some of the issues that will be presented, we cannot anticipate them all. Nor can we judge how these issues will interact with the economic and technological circumstances that will then prevail.

For example, if America acquires a large number of citizens who celebrate the Sabbath on Friday, this would seem to pose problems for public and private employment as well as for five-day public school weeks. However, if technological and economic changes produce radically new flexibility in the workplace that makes work schedules more autonomous, and new teaching devices that make schools as we know them a much smaller part of the educational process, then the problems might be minimized. On the other hand, if international competition makes the workplace more rigid and regimented, and creates a demand for even longer school days, weeks, and years, the problems might then be intensified. We can speculate, but we do not know enough to do so very exactly.

But what does seem certain is that the ultimate fate of the national perspective will not be determined in a vacuum. Underlying social and economic developments of a fundamental sort impacted the pattern of pluralism that supported the twentieth century's nationalization of liberty. Such developments, the context of judicial activism, will continue to shape and ultimately validate constitutional perspectives in the years to come.

---

seeks to use the public authorities to remove trespassers only when they are non-White that law enforcement and the courts should be closed to him? Nevertheless, the case certainly provided a rationale for undermining public enforcement of the discriminatory preferences of private business owners in the South of the 1960s had the Court been required to find one.

Selected Bibliography

I. BOOKS

Abraham, Henry. *Freedom and the Court: Civil Rights and Liberties in the United States*. New York: Oxford University Press, 1967.

Ackerman, Bruce. *We the People*, vol. 1 "Foundations." Cambridge, Mass.: Harvard University Press, 1991

—. *We the People*, vol. 2 "Transformations." Cambridge, Mass.: Harvard University Press, 1998.

Areeda, Phillip. *Antitrust Analysis*, 3rd ed. Boston, Mass.: Little Brown and Co., 1981.

Armor, David. *Forced Justice: School Desegregation and the Law*. New York: Oxford University Press, 1995.

Badgehot, Walter. *The English Constitution*. Ithaca, N.Y.: Cornell University Press, 1966.

Bass, Jack. *Unlikely Heroes*. New York: Simon and Schuster, 1981.

Berger, Raoul. *Government by Judiciary: The Transformation of the Fourteenth Amendment*. Cambridge, Mass.: Harvard University Press, 1977.

Berman, Paul, ed. *Debating PC*. New York: Dell Publishing, 1992.

Berry, Wendell. *Sex, Economy, Freedom and Community*. New York: Pantheon, 1993.

Blasi, Vincent, ed. *The Burger Court: The Counter-Revolution that Wasn't*. New York: Yale University Press, 1983.

Bollinger, Lee. *The Tolerant Society*. New York: Oxford University Press, 1986.

Brison, Susan J., and Walter Sinnott-Armstrong. *Contemporary Perspectives on Constitutional Interpretation.* Boulder, Colo.: Westview Press, 1993.

Burnham, Walter Dean. *Critical Elections and the Mainsprings of American Politics.* New York: W. W. Norton and Co., 1970.

Coll, Steve. *The Deal of the Century: The Breakup of AT & T.* New York: Atheneum, 1986.

Cooper, Phillip J. *Hard Judicial Choices: Federal District Court Judges and State and Local Officials.* New York: Oxford University Press, 1988.

Dahl, Robert A. *Democracy and Its Critics.* New Haven, Conn.: Yale University Press, 1989.

Dixon, Robert G., Jr. *Democratic Representation.* New York: Oxford University Press, 1968.

Drucker, Peter F. *The New Realities.* New York: Harper and Row, 1989.

Dworkin, Ronald. *Taking Rights Seriously,* Cambridge, Mass.: Harvard University Press, 1977.

Ely, John Hart. *Democracy and Distrust.* Cambridge, Mass.: Harvard University Press, 1980.

Emerson, Thomas. *Toward a General Theory of the First Amendment.* New York: Vintage Books, 1966.

Fischer, David Hackett. *Albion's Seed: Four British Folkways in America.* New York: Oxford University Press, 1989.

Fish, Stanley. *There's No Such Thing as Free Speech . . . and It's a Good Thing Too!* New York: Oxford University Press, 1994.

Goldstein, Leslie Friedman. *In Defense of the Text.* Savage, Md.: Rowman & Littlefield, 1991.

Halpern, Stephen C. *On the Limits of the Law: The Ironic Legacy of Title VI of the 1964 Civil Rights Act.* Baltimore: Johns Hopkins University Press, 1994.

Harris, Robert. *The Search for Equality.* Baton Rouge: Louisiana State University Press, 1960.

Hartz, Louis. *The Liberal Tradition in America.* New York: Harcourt, Brace, 1955.

Hirsch, Fred. *Social Limits to Growth.* Cambridge: Harvard University Press, 1977.

Hacker, Andrew *The End of the American Era.* New York: Atherton, 1970.

Hirsch, H. N. *A Theory of Liberty.* New York: Routledge, 1992.

Horn, Robert A. *Groups and the Constitution.* New York: AMS Press, 1956.

Horowitz,Donald. *The Courts and Social Policy*. Washington, D.C.: Brookings Institution, 1977.
Hunter, James Davison. *Culture Wars: The Struggle to Define America.* New York: Basic Books, 1991.
James, Joseph. *The Framing of the Fourteenth Amendment.* Urbana, Ill.: University of Illinois Press, 1956.
Kelly, Alfred H., Winfred A. Harbison, and Herman Belz. *The American Constitution. : its origins and development.* New York: W. W. Norton, 1991.
Kosmin,Barry A., and Seymour P. Lachman.*One Nation Under God: Religion in Contemporary Society.* New York: Harmany Books, 1993.
Lasser, William. *The Limits of Judicial Power.* Chapel Hill: University of North Carolina Press, 1988.
Legler, J. *Toleration and the Reformation.* 2 Vols. New York: Association Press, 1960.
Levinson, Sanford. *Constitutional Faith.* Princeton, N.J.: Princeton University Press, 1988.
Lewis, Anthony. *Make No Law: The Sullivan Case and the First Amendment.* New York: Random House, 1991 .
Lind, Michael. *The Next American Nation.* New York: Free Press, 1995.
Matsuda, Mari et al. *Words that Wound.* Boulder, Colo.: Westview Press, 1993.
Melnick, R. Shep. *Regulation and the Courts: The Case of the Clean Air Act* . Washington, D.C.: Brookings Institution, 1983.
Montagu, Ashley. *The Concept of Race.* Glencoe, Ill.: Free Press of Glencoe, 1964).
Montagu, Ashley. *Man's Most Dangerous Myth: The Fallacy of Race.* New York: Oxford University Press, 1974.
Neely, Richard. *How the Courts Govern America.* New Haven, Conn.: Yale University Press, 1981.
Perry, Michael J. *The Constitution, The Courts and Human Rights.* New Haven, Conn.: Yale University Press, 1982.
Phillips, Kevin. *The Emerging Republican Majority.* New Rochelle, N.Y.: Arlington House, 1969.
Portes, Alejandro, and Ruben G. Rumbaut. *Immigrant America: A Portrait.* Berkeley: University of California Press, 1990.
Rausch, Jonathan. *Kindly Inquisitors.* Chicago: University of Chicago Press, 1993.
Riker, William. *Democracy in the United States.* New York: Macmillan, 1963.

Roche, John P. *Courts and Rights.* New York: Random House, 1966.

—. *The Quest for the Dream.* New York: Macmillan, 1963.

Rosenberg, Gerald N. *The Hollow Hope: Can Courts Bring about Social Change?* Chicago: University of Chicago Press, 1991.

Schwartz, Herman. *The Burger Years* . New York: Penguin Books, 1987.

Shapiro, Martin.*Freedom of Speech.* Englewood Cliffs, N.J.: Prentice-Hall, 1966.

Simon, Herbert. *Administrative Behavior.* New York: Macmillan, 1947.

Smith, Christopher E. *Courts and Public Policy.* Chicago: Nelson-Hall, 1993.

Sunstein, Cass. *Democracy and the Problem of Free Speech..* New York: Free Press, 1993.

—. *The Partial Constitution.* Cambridge, Mass.: Harvard University Press, 1993.

Swanson, Wayne R. *The Christ Child Goes to Court.* Philadelphia: Temple University Press, 1990.

TenBroek, Jacobus. *Equal Under Law.* New York: Collier Books, 1965.

Tocqueville, Alexis de. *Democracy in America.* 2 Vol. New York: Vintage Books, 1945.

Tushnet, Mark, editor.*The Warren Court in Historical and Political Prespective.* Charlottesville: University Press of Virginia, 1993.

Vose, Clement. *Caucasians Only: The Supreme Court, the N.A.A.C.P., and the Restrictive Covenant Cases.* Berkeley: University of California Press, 1959.

Weiss, Michael J. *The Clustering of America.* New York: Harper and Row, 1988.

Wills, Gary. *Under God: Religion and American Politics.* New York: Simon and Schuster, 1990.

Wood, Robert. *Remedial Law.* Amherst, Mass.: University of Massachusetts Press, 1990.

II. ARTICLES

Ackerman, Bruce. "Constitutional Politics/Constitutional Law." *Yale Law Journal* 99 (1989): 453.

Bickel, Alexander. "The Original Understanding and the Segregation Decision."*Harvard Law Review* 69 (1955): 1.

Brest, Paul. "The Fundamental Rights Controversy: Essential Contradictions of Normative Constitutional Scholarship," *Yale Law Journal* 90 (1981): 1063.

Caldeira, G., and J. Wright. "Organized Interests and Agenda Setting in the U.S. Supreme Court." *American Political Science Review* (December 1988): 1109-1127.

Casper, Jonathan A. "The Supreme Court and National Policy Making," *American Political Science Review* 60 (March 1976): 50.

Chayes, Abram. "The Role of the Judge in Public Law Litigation." *Harvard Law Review* 89 (1976): 1281.

—. "The Supreme Court 1981 Term, Foreward, Public Law Litigation and the Burger Court." *Harvard Law Review* 96 (1982): 4

Cox, Archibald. "Foreword: Constitutional Adjudication and the Promotion of Human Rights." *Harvard Law Review* 80 (1966): 1.

Dahl, Robert A. "Decision-Making in a Democracy: The Supreme Court as a National Policy-Maker." *Journal of Public Law*. 6 (Fall 1957): 279.

Dworkin, Ronald. Review of Fried, Charles, *Order and Law: Arguing the Reagan Revolution—A Firsthand Account.* (New York: Simon and Schuster, 1991) in *The New York Review of Books* 38, no.13 (July 18, 1991): 23.

Frantz, L. B. "Congressional Power to Enforce the Fourteenth Amendment Against Private Acts." 73*Yale Law Journal* 1353 (1964).

Graham, Howard J. "Our 'Declaratory' Fourteenth Amendment." 7 *Stanford Law Review* 7 (1954): 3.

Hackman, J. "Lobbying the Supreme Court: An Appraisal of Political Science Folklore."*Fordham Law Review* 35 (1966): 15.

Halpern, Stephen. "On the Imperial Judiciary and Comparative Institutional Development and Power in America." In *Supreme Court Activism and Restraint,* edited by Stephen C. Halpern and Charles M. Lamb. Lexington, Mass.: Lexington Books, 1982.

Mendelsohn, Wallace. "The Politics of Judicial Activism," *Emory Law Journal* 24 (1975): 43.

Michelman, Frank. "Foreword: On Protecting the Poor Through the Fourteenth Amendment," *Harvard Law Review* 83(1969): 7.

Nelson, R. "The Eighteenth-Century Background of John Marshall's Constitutional Jurisprudence,"*Michigan Law Review* 76 (1978): 893.

Post, Robert C. "William J. Brennan and the Warren Court" in *The Warren Court in Historical and Political Perspective,* Mark Tushnet, ed. Charlottesville: University Press of Virginia, 1993.

Roelofs, Joan. "Judicial Activism as Social Engineering: A Marxist Interpretation of the Warren Court." In *Supreme Court*

Activism and Restraint, edited by Stephen C. Halpern and Charles M. Lamb. Lexington, Mass: Lexington Books, 1982.

Roche, John. "American Liberty: An Examination of the Tradition of Freedom." In his *Shadow and Substance.* New York: Collier Books, 1964.

—."We've Never Had More Freedom." In his *Shadow and Substance.* New York: Collier Books, 1964.

Shapiro, Martin. "Fathers and Sons: the Court, the Commentators and the Search for Values." In *The Burger Court: The Counter-Revolution that Wasn't,* Vincent Blasi, ed. New York: Yale University Press, 1983.

Vose, Clement. "Litigation as a Form of Pressure Group Activity." *Annals of the American Academy of Political and Social Science* 319 (1958): 20.

—."The National Consumers League and the Brandeis Brief." *Midwest Journal of Political Science* 1 (1957): 276.

Wechsler, Herbert, "Toward Neutral Principles of Constitutional Law." *Harvard Law Review* 73 (1959): 1.

Wolfe, Alan. "The Return of the Melting Pot." *The New Republic,* (December 31, 1990.)

III. GOVERNMENT DOCUMENTS

Congressional Globe of the 39th Congress, 1st Session, 1865.

Congressional Globe of the 42nd Congress, 1st Session, Appendix, 1872.

Federal and State Constitutions, Colonial Charters and Other Organic Laws of the States, Territories and Colonies Now or Heretofore forming the United States of America, Volumes I through VII. F. N. Thorpe, ed. Washington, D.C.: Government Printing Office, 1909.

Federal and State Constitutions, Colonial Charters and Other Organic Laws of the United States. B. P. Poore, ed. Washington, D.C.: Government Printing Office, 1877.

Index Digest of State Constitutions. Albany, N.Y.: New York State Constitutional Commission, 1915.

Index

About the Author

Frederick Lewis is Professor of Political Science at the University of Massachusetts Lowell. He holds a law degree from Harvard and a political science doctorate from Tufts.

For over twelve years he served as Chair of the Department of Political Science; in recent years he has been an occasional labor arbitrator and a consultant/reviewer for the United States Department of Education. He is the author of *The Dilemma in the Enforcement of the Fourteeth Amendment* and the *Nationalization of Liberty.*